A Light Walk

ROCK LIGHTHOUSES OF BRITAIN
– the end of an era?
Christopher Nicholson

This book vividly recounts the history of thirteen rock lighthouses
in various parts of the British Isles. It is full of intriguing information
and is profusely illustrated with line drawings, diagrams and
dramatic photographs.

". . . a well crafted, well illustrated and fascinating account of these seaway lights . . ."
Books in Scotland

". . . this enjoyable book is packed with dramatic illustrations and photographs
and detailed accounts of the construction and history to the present day . . ."
The Geographical Magazine

ISBN 1-870325-41-9

NO MORE PARAFFIN-OILERS
Ian Cassells

'Paraffin-Oiler' was the nickname for a Scottish lightkeeper and
Ian Cassells, a former lightkeeper, provides a light-hearted and true
account of life in the Lighthouse Service through personal
reminiscences and tales from colleagues.

" . . . an absorbing account of Scottish lighthouses laced with humour
and tales of courage."
The Northern Times

ISBN 1-870325-21-4

A QUIET LIFE
Martha Robertson

This is the story of a child growing up in the 20s and 30s in the
unusual environment that constitutes a lighthouse station — a way of
life that has disappeared forever. The author also describes the war years
and life in the Wrens and brings to her story a delightful warmth with
more than a touch of humour.

ISBN 1-870325-71-0

A Light Walk

Ian Cassells

Illustrations by Sarah Jane Adams

Whittles Publishing

Published by:
Whittles Publishing
Roseleigh House
Latheronwheel
Caithness KW5 6DW
Scotland

ISBN 1 870325 51 6

Designed by Janet Watson

Printed by BPC-AUP Aberdeen Ltd.

Contents

Foreword

 THIS narrative was written some time ago after I had completed my lighthouse walk. After one or two half-hearted attempts to get it published, the manuscript then languished, half-forgotten at the back of my wardrobe.

Recently my *No More Paraffin-Oilers* was published by Whittles Publishing and is proving so popular that Keith Whittles suggested another book about lighthouses to me. It was then I remembered the manuscript of *Light Walk*.

As the events recorded in *Light Walk* occurred back in 1986, my initial plan was to try and edit and update the manuscript, but each time I tried it seemed to me that the story lost some of its spontaneity. Finally, I gave up and decided to leave the story in the original form as it was first written during the long, winter night watches at Stroma lighthouse. To help bring the reader up-to-date, I have included an afterword at the end of the narrative.

Ian Cassells
Scrabster

Rudolph Hess and the Muckle Flugga

 THE initial urge for me to do a long distance walk of some description, was inadvertently inspired by the ex-Nazi deputy leader Rudolf Hess.

I shall explain. At the time I was serving as a lightkeeper at Muckle Flugga, the lighthouse situated on the northernmost piece of real estate in the British Isles. The 'Flugga' is the largest of a group of small islets, skerries, stacks and barren rocks which are collectively known as the Holms of Burrafirth, and are situated about a quarter of a mile offshore from the headland and bird sanctuary of Hermaness on the island of Unst, the northernmost of the Shetland Islands. In fact, many people may not realize it, but this part of Britain is actually situated geographically nearer the Arctic circle than Cape Farewell in Greenland, the northern cities of Bergen and Leningrad, or the Alaskan peninsula.

The lighthouse was built here at this remote outpost as a result of the Crimean war, when it was envisioned that British warships would frequently be passing through the area as they kept up their blockade of the Russian Baltic fleet. I was there because I had been appointed assistant lightkeeper by the Northern Lighthouse Board for whom I worked. My working routine consisted of spending twenty-eight days manning the lighthouse, in company with two other lightkeepers, followed by twenty-eight days ashore at the lighthouse shore station at Burrafirth, Unst, where my wife and young daughter lived.

At such an isolated and weather-beaten lighthouse, there was always plenty of general maintenance work to keep us busy. However, to help occupy our spare time and the dreary long northern nights, the Shetland public library, based in Lerwick, would periodically send out to us via our relief boat, three, stout wooden boxes packed with a fairly miscellaneous selection of library books. It was amongst one of these welcome consignments that I happened to come across a book about the late Herr Hess. I read with interest about his enigmatic flight to Britain, and his subsequent long incarceration in Berlin's Spandau prison after the war had ended. I read that to help combat the boredom of his daily prison exercise period, Hess would picture in his mind's eye that he was merrily hiking through the pre-war German countryside, rather than face the prosaic reality of wearily trudging around the gardens of Spandau prison under the watchful gaze of his multinational guards.

Now, although I am not equating a month on Muckle Flugga with life imprisonment in Spandau, there is a certain similarity with respect to the confinement. In fact Hess was better off as he had more room in which to walk around. My lighthouse station consisted of little more than the light-tower itself; an accommodation building containing the bedrooms, living room and kitchen occupied by the three keepers manning the light; the engine room, housing our three generators and radio equipment; a pocket handkerchief of a courtyard; and an equally Lilliputian-proportioned helicopter landing pad. The whole lot was perched precariously upon the flattened summit of the craggy, steep-sided rock called Muckle Flugga.

Spending almost a month at a time in such a confined area, lack of exercise can become a problem, and with a well-stocked freezer, the waist line soon spreads. In fact, I remember one of my fellow light keepers telling me that he could quite often put on as much as a stone in weight during the course of his duty spell. This extra weight he would duly lose when leading a more active life during his off-duty month ashore on Unst. In an attempt to tackle this problem, I got into the habit of taking a daily walk down the steep, cliff-hanging stairway which led to sea level and the natural rock jetty where our relief boat landed. This was a descent and therefore ascent of about two hundred steps each way. At first this was fine, and I would some times go up and down as many as three times, working up a good, healthy sweat under the watchful and slightly bemused gaze of the numerous puffins, razorbills and guillemots who nested on the rock every year. However, the daily trip soon became monotonous, and then as the winter set in and the weather began to deteriorate, it became too dangerous. Massive rollers would come crashing between Muckle Flugga and an adjacent stack, shooting swirling white, freezing water up the stairway and filling the air with foam and spray. Then I discovered the library book, and resolved to emulate Herr Hess.

From a starting point at the entrance door of the accommodation building, I paced out a route which took me across the cobbled courtyard; around the outside of the engine room and light-tower; the full circumference of the helicopter pad; along the narrow path which led off the helicopter pad and ran the length of the accommodation building and led me back to my starting point at the entrance door. I estimated that twelve of these circuits would measure roughly one mile, and every day from that day onwards, I would nip out after dinner and do at least thirty-six circuits, often more, depending on weather and inclination, but always nothing less than a good three mile walk.

. . . and resolved to emulate Herr Hess . . .

Of course these antics did not go unnoticed by my fellow keepers, and they would occasionally chip in with such gems of wit as: "I am sure there must be a quicker way of digging a trench around the place", as they watched me striding round on my daily circuits. All the comments in the world could not have bothered me, because inside my head I was not on Muckle Flugga but back on the Scottish mainland, steadily walking from my home town of Thurso, Lands End bound.

I happened to explain what I was doing one day to my good mate and fellow assistant lightkeeper Davie Macdonald. He was quite tickled by the idea, but plagued me for weeks by asking if I was at Golspie yet. Davie was a native of the small Sutherlandshire town. On completing what was about the fifteenth lap of the circuit one day, I yelled through the open accommodation doorway, that by my reckoning I had just passed Dunrobin Castle and I was about to enter Golspie. I heard a heavy sigh from within and a plaintive, forlorn voice shouted: "Have a pint in the Sutherland Arms for me, will you!"

When my tour of duty was done, I would return to the lighthouse shore station at Burrafirth and the welcome company of my wife Hilary and daughter Roxanne. As I have never been, nor ever had any inclination to be, a car driver, walking was my customary mode of transport when ashore. The island of Unst had a fairly scattered community, and the nearest shop from the shore station was a good two miles distant along a winding, single track road which passed alongside the beautiful golden yellow sands of Burrafirth beach and then through rough moorland where herds of inquisitive Shetland ponies would be turned out to graze in summer. This was a walk which I enjoyed, and one which I would make with little more excuse than going to the shop to collect the weekly local paper, the excellent *Shetland Times*.

The nearest pub was all of five miles from Burrafirth, and every Sunday dinner time when I was ashore, I would take my cross-collie dog Storm, and hike the ten mile round trip for the sake of a couple of pints of beer. In fact, after some time I had this particular journey so off pat, that I could leave the shore station at a certain time and arrive at the pub dead on opening time. After the five mile slog, boy, did that first pint taste good!

As I walked along Unst's roads, drivers would frequently stop and offer me a lift, but unless it was a particularly foul day of weather, I seemed to be time after time politely declining their offers. I found myself discovering that I derived a great deal of quiet enjoyment out of just simply walking.

Life changes, and lightkeepers are transferred to different lighthouses. In the March of 1985 I was transferred to Stroma lighthouse in the Pentland Firth, with my mainland living accommodation at the one-man operated lighthouse of Holborn Head at Scrabster, near Thurso. I was thoroughly delighted with this move, as my parents lived in Thurso and I had been brought up in the town and had many old friends living in the area. Sadly however, my elation was short-lived, as during my first term of duty on Stroma island, I received the earth-shattering news that my wife Hilary had been killed.

With the obvious shock of my wife's death came the realization that I now had to reassess my entire future life, particularly regarding the welfare of my daughter Roxanne, who at the time was only five years old. My initial reaction was that I would have to resign from the lighthouse service in order that I could look after her full-time. But at this point my parents stepped in. They said that they would be more than willing to look after Roxanne for me while I was away on duty at the lighthouse, and they quite logically pointed out to me that she had never known anything other than her dad disappearing to the lighthouse every second month, and the folly of throwing away a good job in such times of high unemployment.

Indeed, my parents were a great comfort and very understanding in those early, bad days, and have ever since provided Roxanne with a more stable and far better upbringing than I would ever have been capable of doing by myself. She still remains the one very special person who I look forward greatly to seeing each time I return ashore.

On the island of Stroma — the name derives from the Norse *Straumey* which translates as *the island in the stream*, the stream being the fiercely turbulent Pentland Firth — there is plenty of room for walking.

Unlike the cramped rock of Muckle Flugga, Stroma is a sizeable island, roughly three miles long by a mile wide at the widest part. The island was quite populously inhabited up until the early 1960s when a tragically ironic mass migration took place. The islanders had long complained that they badly required a good, safe harbour at the south end of the island. Eventually the 'powers that be' assented and funds were provided for the construction of a sheltered harbour. There was little or no work on Stroma apart from subsistence crofting and fishing. Over the previous decade many islanders had left for the mainland, but the majority of able-bodied men left remaining were more than happy to be employed by the contractors in helping to build the new harbour. However, when work on the 'Haven' was completed, these men discovered that they had all earned sufficient money in wages to enable them to take their families and quit the hard life on Stroma and go and live on the Caithness mainland where they could get a well-paid job at the new Atomic Energy Research Station at Dounreay.

To walk around the island nowadays can be a melancholy and slightly eerie experience. Everywhere one looks there are signs of deserted habitation. Abandoned crofts and houses, some still in quite good condition. There is even an old G.P.O. phone box, it's post office red paintwork beginning to fade and peel. There is not a soul in sight and the only sounds to be heard are the harsh roar of the Firth and the mocking screech of the ever-wheeling gulls.

One night in early January 1986, I was lying in my bed at the lighthouse on Stroma, snugly and complacently listening to the howling banshee of a full-blooded Pentland Firth gale which was accompanied by the staccato rapping of hail, rain and sea spray on the glass of my bedroom window. Half asleep, I found my mind wandering and thinking back on the days at Muckle Flugga and my daily walk on my imaginary trip from Thurso to Lands End. (I think that I had reached Birmingham by the time I was transferred). 'Wouldn't it be something,' I mused, 'to be able to do such a walk for real.' Realistically though I realized that this was likely to remain a pipedream at least at the present time, due to work commitments. True enough, many people have walked from John O'Groats to Lands End well within the four weeks off-duty time which I would have available, but I would not be out to break records, I would rather take my time and enjoy myself than be subject to a daily regimen of as many miles in the shortest time possible. Anyway, walking from John O'Groats to Lands End was becoming pretty hackneyed, and I began to wonder if I could come up with an idea for some kind of walk which was different and original. Not necessarily something spectacular, but something which I could accomplish which would fit in with the demands of my job. Then the idea suddenly hit me!

The year 1986 was the bicentenary of the founding of the lighthouse authority, the Northern Lighthouse Board, who are responsible for the lighthouses in Scotland and the Isle of Man, as opposed to the sister service of Trinity House who deal with England. I was aware that our headquarters in Edinburgh was determined to make something of an occasion of the anniversary, which was quite understandable. After all it is not every day you get to celebrate a two hundredth birthday. I wondered what if I was to suggest that to celebrate and help publicize the bi-centenary, some idiot did a walk around Scotland's coast and called at each of the manned mainland lighthouses on the way. Of course, yours truly was more than willing to be the idiot in question.

I was a long time getting to sleep that night as I lay plotting and scheming various routes, logistics, etc., and how I might best present the idea to my bosses.

The following afternoon I made two 'phone calls. The first call I made was to my mother in Thurso to sound her out about a matter of conscience. I had worked out that such a trip as the one which I was planning would take me about nine weeks to complete, and I was feeling guilty about being away from my daughter for that long, thinking that I was perhaps being a bit selfish. My mother assured me not to worry, as during the coming summer they had been planning on going on holiday, and this would fall during the time I had proposed for my walk.

The second 'phone call I made was to lighthouse headquarters in George Street, Edinburgh. Here I spoke to Mr. Clark, who was the administration officer responsible for all matters relating to the bi-centenary celebrations. I think he was a bit bemused when I suddenly sprung my proposal upon him, but he heard me out and suggested that I write a detailed letter fully outlining my plan. However, he added, that he honestly did not know what kind of reception such a suggestion would receive.

With the aid of a large AA road atlas, I spent the next few days working out a feasible route which would enable me to call at the twenty or so manned lighthouses scattered around the Scottish coast, and the estimated time it would take me to complete this course. I then drafted a letter containing all this information and the proposed aims of the walk. Finally I pointed out that should this all be approved, a month's leave of absence would be required to give sufficient time to do the entire trip in one go. As I would already have two off-duty months ashore, this additional month would give me a total of twelve weeks, which I considered would be ample time. I posted the letter immediately I arrived ashore from Stroma, and patiently awaited the reply.

The weeks passed quickly by and it was soon almost time for me to return to duty. By this time I had all but given up waiting for a reply to my letter, quite convinced that my suggestion had ended up in the waste basket. Then a familiar buff envelope from 84, George Street arrived in the post one afternoon. I cannot recall the exact wording, but the letter stated something to the effect that at a meeting of the Northern Lighthouse Board Bi-Centennial Committee, my idea had been discussed. All present were in agreement that I be given the go-ahead providing that a relief could be found for my requested month off. Good luck.

Preparation and the off

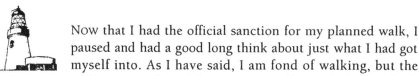

World Cup and blisters . . .

Now that I had the official sanction for my planned walk, I paused and had a good long think about just what I had got myself into. As I have said, I am fond of walking, but the shortest possible route which I had provisionally worked out which would include all the Scottish manned coastal lighthouses, covered a walking distance of 1,200 miles. The furthest I had ever walked in my life, had been my regular Sunday ten mile round trip to the nearest pub, when I had lived on the island of Unst. I consider that I am usually reasonably fit, but it was patently obvious to me that I would have to put in some pretty serious training in the three month grace I had before I was due to start the walk at the beginning of June. There was little I could do that week as I was due to fly back out to Stroma in a couple of days, so I took the course of action which I usually take when faced with a subject or dilemma about which I know little or nothing. I went down to the local public library and took out a number of books on long distance walking.

Thinking back on it, over the course of the next couple of weeks I must have read at least ten different books on the subject of walking. I did manage to glean the odd gem of really useful information, but the majority of specialized advice just appeared to me to be a simple matter of plain common sense. One thing which I did find, was the fact that each author and self-proclaimed expert seemed to have their very own definite and quite set views about walking, and from book to book these could be vastly contradictory. There was one particular example of this which quite amused me at the time. One quite reputed expert repeatedly stressed throughout his book the importance of good foot hygiene, e.g. the washing of feet every night, application of foot powder and regular changes of socks. In complete contradiction to this, another writer — who should know what he was talking about, as this man had completed some truly marathon walks — advocated that he liked to wear his socks until they literally rotted on his feet!

This problem of contrasting information was not new to me. When I had lived in Shetland, my wife and I kept a couple of horses and we found the same kind of set ideas and contradictions in the vast amount of equine literature on the market. I resolved to do exactly what I used to do then. Use the information from the books as a rough guideline, but do whatsoever I found suited myself and the circumstances best.

As soon as I was back on duty at Stroma lighthouse I began the physical training side of my preparations in earnest. The lighthouse station is situated at the extreme northern tip of the island, overlooking the notorious Swilkie whirlpool, and covering the narrow channel of swirling water between Stroma and Orkney, which the shellbacks of the old sailing ships used to call "Hell's Mouth". From the lighthouse to the harbour at the Haven on the island's southern coast, was a distance of two and a half miles following a rough and bumpy single track road. This gave a return trip of five miles, and I began to walk this route at least once a day, and frequently as many as three or four times. When I fancied a bit of variety, I would take to the clifftops and walk right around the island.

First thing in the morning and last thing at night, I would rub my feet with vinegar to toughen them up. However, after a week or so, and socks smelling like fish and chip suppers, I put the vinegar back into the pantry and took to using surgical spirit.

During the quiet moments on the long night watches, I would sit and pore over the maps relevant to the walk. I worked and reworked my proposed route, estimating daily mileages and possible overnight stopping places. I had at first thought to set myself a daily target of twenty-five miles, but changed this to a day's walking and a likely overnight stop, such as somewhere I knew I could get a bed for the night, or as I intended taking a light tent with me, somewhere suitable to camp.

Suitable equipment was something else which I had to consider. Obviously a good pair of boots was the chief priority, but I was also going to need durable and light waterproof clothing; a suitable backpack; light tent; and a sleeping bag, just for starters. I decided to not bother carrying cooking gear, meaning to rely on meals on a 'catch as catch can' basis.

When I had finally drawn up a list of what essential equipment I would require, I realized that these things were going to cost me a fair bit of money, which is a particular commodity I rarely have in abundance, or for very long. Easy, I thought, I will do what all the top expeditions do, write to the various firms which supply or manufacture the type of equipment which I was in need of, and ask them if they would kit me out by way of sponsorship. "There's bound to be a rush for the honour of being involved in this enterprise", I thought. Since the Northern

Lighthouse Board is essentially a Scottish organization, and my walk was to be confined to the Scottish mainland, I decided to be patriotic and give the relevant Scottish firms the first chance to back me.

All the replies I received wished me the best of luck in my endeavour, but good wishes was all I received. I would have to equip myself as cheaply as possible out of my own scanty pocket.

The following four weeks on Stroma were fairly eventful. I spent most of my spare time in training, walking back and forth from the landing to the lighthouse; reading more books on walking, and studying my road maps for ways to shave miles off my route.

On returning ashore, I immediately set out about the business of scouring the Thurso shops for a good pair of boots. Here I struck lucky. A local shop called 'Leisure Activities', ran by a very helpful young couple, sold me an excellent pair of light hiking boots of Italian manufacture. When I had explained what I wanted the boots for, the couple had gone off into a huddle in a corner where they had a hurried, whispered conversation between themselves which resulted in my being offered a very generous discount on the purchase of the boots. Thank you 'Leisure Activities' — I promised I would mention your name if I ever came to write about my enterprise.

I was determined to break in my new boots as soon as possible, and the following morning I set out from my home at Scrabster to walk to the nearby village of Halkirk, a round trip of about twelve miles. Despite a bitter north wind and the occasional sleet shower, it was a pleasant enough walk through the flat Caithness countryside, past road verges dotted with clumps of snowdrops and splashed with the yellow and purple of flowering crocus. Most satisfying of all was the fact that my new boots caused me no problems or the slightest discomfort whatsoever. In fact all the training walks I carried out wearing those boots, I was never inflicted with as much as one tiny blister. The only blisters I suffered during the actual walk itself, occurred during the first week and were a direct result of my own stupidity and not due to the boots.

Over the course of the next couple of weeks ashore, I must have tramped all over the western half of the county. Heading due west I would walk out to the bustling, ultra-modern, nuclear complex of Dounreay, and then head home along twisting country back roads which took me past fields in which were sited ancient chambered cairns and standing stones overgrown with moss and grass and the handiwork of far earlier inhabitants of Caithness. I wondered what the pre-Iron Age people would have made of the glistening, light-blue painted dome of the experimental fast reactor at Dounreay. Other days I would head east along the windswept northern coast to the village of Castletown, and again following the little-used back roads, return to Thurso, passing on the way long abandoned flagstone quarries which in the past were the chief basis of this side of the county's economy and prosperity.

By the time my final week ashore came round, I felt quite capable of tackling the hike of twenty-three miles to the county town of Wick. This walk would be an important test, as I predicted that this distance would pretty well work out at my daily average during the walk itself.

A sunny spring morning saw me leave Scrabster at nine o'clock in the morning, after first leaving my dog Storm with a friend. Storm had accompanied me on all my other practice hikes, but I considered twenty-three miles along the busy main road, a bit unfair on her. Only two miles out of Thurso I nearly came a cropper. I was walking past a field of sheep where newly-born lambs were skipping and cavorting about in the warm sunshine. Glancing into the field, I spotted a lamb's head apparently sprouting out of the ground. The wee creature was bleating plaintively, while a rather concerned and perplexed looking ewe, probably the mother, looked on. It seemed that the ground had either subsided suddenly at that spot, or more likely, that the lamb had fallen into a pothole. As there was no farmer in sight to whom I could point out the plight of the beast, I vaulted over the fence to free the lamb myself. Much to my amusement I hauled the lamb out only to find that the pothole was deeper than I had thought, and the lamb which I had rescued had been standing on the back of one of his companions who must have fallen down the hole earlier. Stooping down, I stretched out and caught the animal by the scruff of the neck and hauled it into the daylight, only to feel at the same time a searing, red-hot, stab of pain across the muscles of my upper back.

Painfully I made my way back to the road, and even more painfully I clambered over the fence surrounding the field. I crossed the road and lay with my back pressed to a flat-walled dyke constructed out of Caithness flagstones; lit a cigarette and soundly cursed potholes, ground subsidence, and chiefly, the obtuse stupidity of the North Country Cheviot sheep. This all helped to make me feel a bit better, and ignoring the beckoning sight of Thurso, still visible on my backtrack, I turned to the east and strode on. Although the occasional sharp twinge of pain activated some terrible language, as the hours and the miles passed by I found the pain becoming number and number, until after a pint of beer at the pub in the village of Watten, some six miles from Wick, it had disappeared altogether.

I finally arrived at my destination a little after four o'clock in the afternoon. Although I had found the last mile a bit hard going, I appeared to have stood up to the walk quite well, and my primary preoccupation was not physical discomfort of any kind, but good honest hunger as I had eaten little since a hearty breakfast early that morning. I purchased a fish and chip supper which I devoured greedily while waiting at the bus station for the next bus back to Thurso, and thought back on the day's performance.

... lit a cigarette and soundly cursed ... the obtuse stupidity of the North Country Cheviot sheep ...

Returning to Thurso by bus that evening, I wryly looked out of the window at the road which had taken me the best part of a day to walk, and which the bus was speeding along, taking half an hour for the same trip. I think it was at that moment when I finally realized why the internal combustion engine had caught on so well.

When I awoke the following morning, I discovered to my concern that I was suffering from an agonizing pain in both ankles, around the region of the Achilles tendon. I had planned on walking to Wick again that day, staying overnight with my sister-in-law who lived in the town, and walking back to Thurso the following morning. This was now quite out of the question, and in fact I found that I could barely walk the two miles into Thurso to see my daughter. Nagging thoughts about my fitness to complete the task I had set myself kept me awake for some time that night. However, next day the pain seemed to have completely disappeared.

That weekend, the last ashore before I was due back out on Stroma, I came by another essential piece of equipment, a backpack. I was enjoying Sunday dinner at my parent's house, when my father produced a distinctly battered 'Campari' backpack, enthusiastically stating: "This will be just the job for you. Your brother Stephen travelled all over Greece with it!"

I warily eyed the backpack with inner misgivings. I already owned a slightly smaller but similar backpack in my house at Scrabster. It had belonged to my late wife, and I had discarded it as not being suitable for a journey such as the one which I was planning. However, not wishing to seem churlish, I gratefully accepted his offer, bearing in mind the old adage, 'beggars can't be choosers'. As things turned out later, like the boots, I had really struck lucky again, and as the walk progressed I began to have quite an affection for that battered backpack.

Tuesday morning dawned and I flew out from Dounreay airstrip in the Bond Helicopters Bolkow BO 105 for my last tour of duty on Stroma before the off. Once I had settled in, I threw myself into the same routine as before, marching back and forth between the lighthouse and the harbour.

By this time the administration staff at Northern Lighthouse Board headquarters had been busy. It had been decided that as well as using the walk to promote the lighthouse bi-centenary, it should also be a sponsored walk in aid of the Royal National Lifeboat Institution. This was a charity which I thought fitted the lighthouse theme particularly well. I found a parcel of sponsor forms awaiting me on Stroma and a letter from Mr. Clark informing me that he had notified the press about the planned walk.

The press were not slow to react, and the following morning I received a 'phone call from Radio West, the local radio station based in Ayr. I did a taped telephone interview with them, mainly explaining which light-houses in their area I would be visiting, and a little of the history of the Northern Lighthouse Board. It was an interview which I am certain I might have made a better job of, but at the time I was a bit concerned about the tatties boiling over as it was my turn to be lighthouse cook that week.

That afternoon I had another lengthy chat with a journalist from the *Scotsman* (surprised that the sex equality gang haven't got them yet, surely it should be the *Scotsperson*?).

It seemed to me that things were really beginning to get off the ground all of a sudden, and that evening I had yet another 'phone call, this time from my mother. She informed me that there was an article about my planned walk in the *Press and Journal*. Quite indignantly she declared: "They have gone and printed your age!" I informed her that this did not particularly bother me. After all, thirty-three is hardly over the hill. Dammit, I'm younger than Bruce Springsteen and Sylvester Stallone! "Well, it bothers me," replied mother. "your daughter thinks that I am only twenty-one!"

Towards the end of that week I received a call from a completely unexpected quarter, Radio Shetland. I say unexpected, because Shetland was obviously not on my route, and I did not think that my head office would have bothered in sending them a press release. I mentioned this to Mary Blance, the station presenter who had called, and I asked her if she had read about the proposed walk in one of the national papers. "Oh no," she replied. "We knew about this weeks ago. I received a nice long letter from Lowrie up at Gutcher telling me all about it and how you were once on Muckle Flugga."

'Lowrie up at Gutcher,' was Lawrence Tulloch, an old friend and ex-lightkeeper. He had left the lighthouse service and become the postmaster at the village of Gutcher on the island of Yell. When I had been working on Muckle Flugga, Lowrie had started up what must be Britain's most northerly local magazine, the *Blue Mull Triangle* (Blue Mull was the name of the sound between the islands of Yell and Unst) to which I had occasionally contributed. How he had found out about the walk, was beyond me, but harkening back to the days when I lived in Shetland, there always seemed to be some remarkable and mysterious bush telegraph at work. The people of Shetland showed a great deal of interest in the affair, and donated very generously to the cause.

Those last four weeks on Stroma seemed to flash by, and in next to no time I was back on board the helicopter, touching down at Dounreay airstrip. As I ran to catch the taxi which would take me home to Holborn Head, Phil Green our helicopter pilot, gave me a farewell wave with the sponsorship form which I had managed to palm off on him. I had just nine days to go before the off.

I set out to buy my last essential purchases, a sleeping bag and a lightweight tent. The sleeping bag proved to be an excellent bargain. It was snug and comfortable, and most important of all, not too bulky and fairly lightweight. Although an expensive brand of sleeping bag, it was slightly flawed and in consequence I managed to buy it for about one third of the price of a bag in perfect condition. I already had an idea of what kind of tent I intended using, and this was a 'Campari' bivouac tent which I had seen advertised. This type of tent suited my purpose as being both cheap and extremely lightweight, and I was able to purchase one from a local camping shop in Thurso. I asked the shop proprietor what he thought of this kind of tent. He ambiguously replied that one never knew with Campari tents, you either got a really good one or a right pig. I must admit that over the course of the next nine weeks I was to develop something of a love hate relationship with mine; principally the latter.

The bivouac and backpack

During the last week before setting off, I completed a couple of final practice walks. I took things fairly easy and did not exceed much more than sixteen miles in one day. I was delighted to discover that my Achilles tendon trouble seemed to have cleared up completely. I principally put this down to my purchasing and using two 'Sorbuthane' pads. These pads are made of a rubbery type of material and are shaped to fit inside the heel of your boots. They are designed to absorb some of the impact your heel receives when it strikes the ground in the course of normal walking or running. I had them recommended to me by a friend who does quite a lot of walking and who had suggested to me that he thought that the pains which I had suffered after my Wick journey, had been caused by the constant jarring of my heels brought about by walking on the hard surface of a metalled road. For all they were to look at, the pads were expensive, but it was money well spent, as the Achilles tendon problem never reappeared again, and I was able to completely discard the pads at Aberdeen.

The day before my departure I had an interview with the local paper, who sent around a gentleman to take my photograph (although I believe it never actually appeared in the paper). I am not a pretty sight at the best of times, but I hate to think that my gloating visage cracked or damaged the photographer's sensitive camera lens.

At last all was ready. My gear was packed, I was as fit as I ever would be, and I had said my farewells to my daughter, parents and friends. My cross-collie dog Storm had been safely lodged with a friend in Scrabster. I was all set to go.

Thursday, the fifth of June dawned. This was the day, which for no particular reason, I had chosen to begin my journey. The previous evening I had carried out a final check of my gear and equipment, and against my better judgement stayed up until one o'clock in the morning watching Scotland play Denmark in their opening football game of the Mexico World Cup, which left me feeling pretty disgusted with myself for staying up so late, with Scotland's one goal defeat and the standard of world cup refereeing.

My headquarters in Edinburgh had provided me with a sort of checklist which I was to hand to the keeper in charge on my arrival at each lighthouse I was to visit, for him to sign. This checklist basically stated the name of the lighthouse visited, the date and time I had arrived there, and finally a space for the signature of the keeper in charge to authenticate it. I was pleased to notice that the person who had arranged for the form to be printed had the foresight to use an extra strong, durable paper.

The first signature was easy enough to obtain, as it merely involved a walk of little more than ten yards to the door of my neighbour Len Fraser who was the principal lightkeeper in charge of Holborn Head lighthouse.

The squat, stubby tower of Holborn Head lighthouse was constructed by order of the Northern Lighthouse Board in 1862. Situated on a low

Holborn Head lighthouse
courtesy Dounreay Nuclear Power Development Establishment

lying headland, the light commands the approaches to nearby Scrabster harbour. Anybody who has travelled on the Orkney ferry St. Ola will recognize the place, as it is the lighthouse which looks down on the ferry as she steams between Scrabster and Stromness. Although there was once a crew of three men and their families living at and manning this lighthouse, the installation of modern technology only required the attendance of one lightkeeper, and Holborn Head is now what is termed a one-man station, soon to go fully automatic altogether. The two houses which used to be occupied by the two Holborn Head assistant light-keepers are now used as the onshore accommodation for the two Stroma assistant lightkeepers. Len duly signed the checksheet, wished me luck, and I was on my way.

I have always enjoyed walking through Scrabster in the early morning as there always seems to be something going on. Fishing boats landing their catch or taking on supplies and ice; a tanker discharging its cargo of oil to the local oil depot; and the place bustling with tourists and traffic awaiting the Orkney ferry.

The village is mentioned in the ancient Norse sagas when it was called Skarabolstaor. The sagas tell us that in the days when the jarls of Orkney ruled in Caithness, William the Lion, king of Scotland, thought to take advantage of the usual feuding which was going on over in Orkney as to who was the rightful jarl. The Scottish king sent his own representative north to declare that Caithness belonged to the Scottish crown. This claim had been a recurring bone of contention for years. Even Macbeth had an unsuccessful battle with the local Vikings disputing the sovereignty of the county. However, the Orkney dispute was speedily won by jarl Harald Maddadarsson, who immediately sailed across the Firth with his men and assailed the stronghold of Skarabolstaor where William the Lion's men had taken refuge. Bishop Jon, a local ecclesiastic, was sent to negotiate with jarl Harald. The jarl duly negotiated in the best Viking fashion, by putting out both the bishop's eyes, and cutting off his tongue. Seeing this, the stronghold promptly capitulated. The story ended happily though. William the Lion's representative quietly disappeared; the Caithness men who had given him shelter, had their wrists slapped and were fined by jarl Harald who then promptly sailed back to Orkney; and the poor, abused bishop had his speech and eyesight miraculously restored at the nearby well of St. Tredwell.

On the outskirts of Scrabster I was stopped by a passer-by who asked me if I was a Canadian! Why this particular nationality, I just cannot fathom, because in an excessive burst of patriotism over Scotland's World Cup bid, I had stuck a large blue and white saltire on the back of my pack. I explained to my inquisitor that I lived little more than a mile away, to which he uttered a disappointed grunt and promptly went about his business.

I followed the clifftop path which took me around the sweep of the sandy bay and into Thurso, the ancient Viking settlement of 'Thor's river', or as some etymologists argue, 'Bull river'. Thurso is a thriving little town owing almost all of its prosperity to the nearby Atomic Research Establishment of Dounreay. Although there has been much controversy over the subject of late, I am personally neither pro nor anti nuclear power. It is something which has been part of my life since I was a child, and I suppose if I was forced to come down off the fence, it would be on the pro side. I did once work at Dounreay for almost two years and hated every moment of it. Not because of the nature of the substance with which we were working, but because after serving eight years in the Royal Navy, I found the work at Dounreay tedious, repetitive and boring. I do not think that I have, for want of a better phrase, the 'factory mentality' which seems necessary to work in a place like that. This probably accounts for why I jumped at the chance of a job as a lightkeeper when it cropped up.

Quickly leaving Thurso behind me, I headed east for the lighthouse at Dunnet Head which was to be my first stop. A bitter cold wind blew over the flat Caithness countryside bringing with it occasional sharp showers of stinging rain, and in one case, hailstones. Flaming June!

I made steady progress, stopping briefly at the village of Castletown which was at one time an important centre of the Caithness flagstone industry. Fine sand blew across the road which ran alongside the sand-dune dotted beach of Dunnet sands. No tourists in residence on the campsites yet I noticed, and in this weather I did not blame them. By mid afternoon I was walking along the lonely twisting road which meanders past rough moorland, peat bog and small lochans, up to the lighthouse at Dunnet Head, situated at the most northerly point on the British mainland. This is a geographical fact even though the tourists have been conned for years into thinking that the most northerly point is at John O'Groats.

With just a couple of miles to go to the lighthouse, I was walking along with my head hunched down to give me some protection from the weather, when I heard a heavily accented voice shouting behind me. "Hey Danskar!" "Hey you Danskar!"

Being mistaken in my home town of Scrabster for a Canadian was bad enough, but to be mistaken for a Dane at Dunnet, was indeed the limit. Especially when taking into consideration the result of the previous evening's World Cup tie. I slowly turned around and glowered. Muttering darkly: "Danskar huh?" I pointedly indicated the St. Andrew's cross on my backpack.

"Ach yes. Wrong bleddy flag," muttered a wiry, aged gent, quite nonplussed, who then dismounted from his equally aged pushbike to walk alongside of me.

It turned out that my companion was a Norwegian who had settled in this part of Caithness many years ago. (Probably came over with Harald Finehair, I thought uncharitably.) He told me that he had a croft locally and was on his way to work on his peat bank. When he discovered that I wasn't just another tourist on his way to visit Dunnet Head and look at the puffins, but actually a serving lightkeeper myself, he kept me entertained by recounting his boyhood in the Lofoten Islands where his father had been in charge of a lighthouse, and the whole family had to act as his assistants on the job. I was quite sorry to see him go when he finally turned off for his peat bank, and I remember thinking to myself at the time that if he was an example of the kind of characters I was likely to meet on my travels, then life would be entertaining indeed.

Built in 1831 under contract by the firm of John Smith, Inverness, Dunnet Head lighthouse is perched atop sheer cliffs, looking out across the treacherous Firth at the equally sheer cliffs of the island of Hoy, of 'Old

Man' fame. There used to be two fog warning towers on the edge of the cliff-top at the lighthouse. The original tower had to be abandoned due to cliff erosion, and threatened to topple into the Pentland Firth for years. I remember a lightkeeper who once worked at Dunnet, who did not get on particularly well with his boss the principal lightkeeper. I was visiting the place and sitting in the lighthouse bothy drinking tea with him one day when he looked at me conspiratorily and said, "You see, I have this idea. What I will do is lure that old bugger into the old fog tower. Once he is in there, I'll activate one of those electronic machines which transmits an ultrasonic sound. A noise pitched beyond the range of the human ear, but of such a frequency that it will loosen the rock of the cliff top. Then bingo! A large splash in the Pentland Firth; no fog tower; and that old bugger is off my back for good. The perfect murder boy! Oh yes, the perfect murder!"

When I was a boy there used to be a principal lightkeeper at Dunnet Head who was quite renowned as a bit of a character. He would quite often show tourists round the light-tower, and it is reliably reported that in reply to comments about how spectacular the view was from the balcony at the top of the tower, he would blandly comment: "Oh yes. On a clear day you can sometimes see the Queen Elizabeth leaving New York harbour."

I would have liked to have lingered longer at Dunnet Head but the day was wearing on and the weather not improving. After bidding farewell to the keepers, I pushed on back down the road, heading for Canisbay where I was going to spend the night as a guest of James Simpson who owns and farms Stroma island, and his family.

I rejoined the main road at Ham, passing the now derelict watermill which many years ago used to produce meal which was shipped to places all over Europe from the small village harbour.

I stopped at the village of Mey for a welcome pint of beer in the Berriedale Arms. It is near this village where the Queen Mother has her Caithness summer retreat at the Castle of Mey. And it was here that I was brought down to earth.

Since leaving Scrabster that morning, I discovered that news of my walk had obviously got around locally. As I plodded along the road, a lot of passing drivers had flashed their lights, tooted their horns or given me a friendly wave of encouragement. This had all made me begin to feel quite the local hero, so when I was asked in the pub if I was a tourist, I nonchalantly replied that I was on a sponsored walk. Had they not read about it in the local paper?

"Oh no, not another bloody sponsored walker!" exclaimed the landlady with some exasperation. "We get them all here. On roller skates, one-wheeled bikes, riding horses, walking backwards . . . and some joker with a giant wheelbarrow was here only last week!"

Seemingly the pub was regularly visited by the John O'Groats to Lands End travellers, and the locals kept me well amused with anecdotes about the various eccentrics they had met who had called in the pub the night before setting off.

I could have stayed longer but I had to press on to my night's lodgings at Burnside, James Simpson's farm. On my arrival I was very warmly welcomed and James's wife Lena cooked me a beautiful and most appreciated meal. After I had eaten, I put my feet up and had a good 'crack' with my host and hostess over a few large tumblers of whisky, and then went off to bed, dog-tired. We had worked out that in all I had walked twenty-six miles that first day. I slept contentedly.

After a very hearty breakfast I made my farewells to James, Lena and their pretty daughter Christine, and I headed off for the lighthouse at nearby Duncansby Head.

Passing through John O'Groats I noticed the first tourist buses of the season heading for the short crossing ferry to Orkney. The Dutchman, Jan de Groot, whom the village is named after, would have approved. He was invited here by the king of Scotland in 1496 to start the first ferry service between the mainland and Orkney. Messrs. Thomas and Bews are carrying on the tradition now with their new ferry the Pentland Venture. (Had to put in a plug for that, because I helped sail her up from the builder's yard in Hull).

The weather had improved considerably since the previous day, the wind had dropped and the sun sparkled on the waters of the Bores of Duncansby, the narrow straits between the mainland and the island of Stroma, which I looked out upon with mixed feelings.

Duncansby, or Dungalsbaer, as it is called in the Norse Orkneyinga saga is where jarl Thorfinn Siguardsson, one of the most powerful and renowned of the jarls of Orkney, kept a permanent fleet of five longships. This was also one of the places where the notorious and irrepressible Viking raider Svein Asleifarson had a farm. People in Caithness still talk about the exploits of 'Sweyn the Pirate', who became involved in numerous daredevil exploits. Just prior to his death by treachery after conducting a successful raid on Dublin, the Orkneyinga saga quotes one of the defeated Irish leaders calling him '. . . the greatest troublemaker known to them in the western lands'. An epitaph which Svein would have appreciated.

Past the small village of Duncansby, a narrow single track road winds up a steep hill to the lighthouse on the headland. This is a popular route with tourists as it leads onto an exhilarating and scenic coastal route. Duncansby Head lighthouse was a by-product of the First World War and the fleet anchorage at nearby Scapa Flow. A temporary fog signal was first erected here in 1914, and was to be eventually replaced with a permanent fog signal and lighthouse in 1924. In the present day Duncansby Head is the control radio station for the lighthouses at Stroma, North Ronaldsay, Copinsay, and Pentland Skerries. On Stroma we speak to the keepers at Duncansby Head three times daily on routine radio calls, so it was of a personal interest to me to be able to put a face to the voices I had so often spoken to over the radio.

The station was bustling with workmen, aided by the keepers, chipping off the years' accumulated layers of lime wash and white paint from the exterior of the lighthouse buildings. I was told that they were chipping back to the original stonework in order to apply a new type of long-lasting paint which would hopefully cut out the yearly task of white washing the buildings. The work was at different stages and at places you could see the

Duncansby Head lighthouse
courtesy Dounreay Nuclear Power Development Establishment

layers of grey-streaked paintwork which dated back to the Second World War when the lightkeepers had been ordered to mix soot with the lime wash in an attempt to make the lighthouse less of a conspicuous landmark for the German bombers.

The previous day when I had visited Dunnet Head, I had made the long walk along the lighthouse road, and had then to retrace my steps to rejoin the main road. After this, I resolved that I would not walk the same road twice again, unless I had no other option, as by doing so I was adding unnecessary and uncalculated mileage onto my journey. So after a welcome cup of tea and a chat, principal lightkeeper Bert Petrie signed my check sheet and gave me a lift back onto the main road, and I was on my way, finally heading south.

I had woken up that morning after my first day's walking, feeling just a little stiff, mainly in my toe joints and about my shoulders the latter due to carrying the unaccustomed backpack which weighed about thirty kilos. This discomfort had caused me a bit of concern at first, but I found that as the day wore on and the miles passed by, my condition improved rather than deteriorated.

The road took me past the village of Freswick, yet another ancient Viking settlement. Facing the sea stood the ruins of Bucholly castle, which some historians have tentatively identified as the site of the Viking stronghold of Lambaborg, which Svein Asleifarson used as a base for various nefarious activities, and as an occasional bolthole when things became too hot. From here I could look along the long, sandy curve of Sinclair's Bay to my next port of call, the lighthouse at Noss Head.

I stopped briefly for lunch - a pint of beer and two packets of crisps — in the public bar of the Sinclair's Bay Hotel in the village of Keiss before heading off and rejoining the main Wick-Thurso road at the similarly named village of Reiss. The traffic had been pretty light on the John O'Groat's road but the road into Wick was quite busy. I was given fresh heart by several motorists who gave me friendly waves and tooted their horns as they passed by.

On the outskirts of Wick I turned off to take the road which would lead me up to Noss Head lighthouse. This single track road passes right through Wick airport, in fact at one point it actually crosses the main runway, and I had to stop and wait by the safety gate as a Loganair Twin-Otter took off.

The approach to the lighthouse was flanked with bushes of yellow flowering gorse amongst which rabbits scurried for cover as I passed. I thought it very appropriate to see such a profusion of these spiky gorse bushes, as this particular shrub was the 'Suaicheantas', or distinguishing emblem of clan Sinclair. Noss Head lighthouse looks down upon the ruins of the clan's ancient strongholds, the twin castles of Sinclair and Girnigoe.

Noss Head lighthouse
courtesy Christopher Nicholson

The lighthouse at Noss Head had a difficult birth. When a lighthouse was first proposed for the Wick area due to the massive increase in shipping concerned with the herring industry, the Northern Lighthouse Board recommended that the light should be established at Sarclet Head, to the south of Wick; but the Elder Brethren of the sister lighthouse authority of Trinity House favoured Noss Head. An argument raged and the Northern Lighthouse Board felt so strongly about the matter that they actually went so far as to petition Queen Victoria. However, the Board of Trade, who were called in to arbitrate, decided in favour of the English authority's selection. The lighthouse was eventually established in 1849.

On my arrival at the lighthouse I was greeted by principal lightkeeper Sandy Strachan and his wife who kindly made me tea and sandwiches. The warmth of their welcome and hospitality was something which I was to find repeated time and time again by my fellow lightkeepers and their families whenever I turned up at a lighthouse. In fact on leaving Noss Head, Sandy pressed a large bag of butterscotch sweeties into my hand, and muttered, "To give you something to chew on while you are on the road."

That night I spent in Wick, a guest of my sister-in-law Isobel. Wick's golden era was during the days of the big herring fisheries, when the Caithness county town was regarded as one of the major herring fishing stations in the country, if not Europe. I have seen old sepia photographs showing the massed ranks of Fifies and Zulus all jammed together in Wick harbour, their masts creating a miniature, leafless forest. The quayside would be jammed packed with barrels full of the 'silver darlings' and the bustle of the travelling gangs of lassies working a season at the herring gutting and packing. Even now Wick is still renowned for fishing, with the local boat 'Boy Andrew' regularly being named as the champion Scottish fishing boat.

After a quiet night in front of Isobel's television, I made an early start in the morning. I intended following the coast road and spending the night at the village of Dunbeath. I would be a week at least before I called in at the next lighthouse on my list, which was the lighthouse at Covesea Skerries, near Lossiemouth. All the other lighthouses on this extreme north-east coastline were now automatic.

The day was warm with little wind, and the Moray Firth glistened in the sunlight, as calm as a millpond. I walked past Whaligoe where there is a flight of stone steps leading steeply down the cliffside to the water, 365 steps in all, one for each day of the year. Off Clyth Ness I could see an off-shore oil rig lying close inshore and looking like the product of an imaginative child's Meccano set.

I had been suffering a bit of discomfort from my right foot and at the old fishing village of Lybster I stopped and took off my boot and sock to investigate the matter further. Only three days on the road and the one problem which I had been most dreading had manifested itself. Blisters! There was one small one forming on my little toe, and a real beauty already established on my big toe.

On all my practice walks, even when my boots had been brand new, I had not suffered from even the slightest sign of a blister, and I ruefully realized that the cause of my present predicament was none other than my own stupidity.

Some time before I had set out on my walk I had 'phoned my younger brother who lives in Aberdeen. My brother Stephen is a keen and quite accomplished long distance and marathon runner, and I thought that he might be able to give me a few tips. He had, and one of the things he had told me not to do was to wear brand new socks. I had given little notice to this particular piece of advice, and all my socks — I wore two pairs at a time, one pair of thin, ordinary ankle socks, over which I wore a pair of thick, sea-boot stockings — were all pristinely new.

When I reached Inverness I washed all of my socks and was never troubled with another blister for the remainder of the walk. At the time though, those blisters caused me quite a bit of grief off and on. The blisters always appeared on my right foot. I was to call this my jinx foot, as later on the journey I developed what I called my 'eighteen-mile toe', because after I had walked roughly this distance, the joint of the big toe on my right foot used to ache, sometimes quite painfully. Throughout the entire journey my left foot gave me no cause for concern whatsoever.

That night I learned by another mistake. On reaching Dunbeath I stopped at a pub called the Inver Arms, and I asked the landlady if there was anywhere nearby where I might be allowed to camp for the night. She replied that if I did not mind sharing a field with a Shetland pony, I might use the field at the rear of the pub. Although I had a little bit of misgiving about the Shetland pony — I had worked with them quite often in their native islands, and although they might look cute, dinky wee things, they can be vicious little buggers with an almost Machiavellian streak of cunning in them — this seemed to be an excellent arrangement. It had been a hot day and I was feeling tired and thirsty, so I sat down on a comfortable bar stool and ordered a pint of beer which tasted so good, and seemed to last such a short time, that I ordered another. Then the Algeria versus Northern Ireland World Cup tie came on the pub television. Well it was only good manners to support a fellow British team making a bid in Mexico, so I had another couple of pints while I enjoyed the match.

Eventually I reluctantly stirred myself to go out into the field and erect my bivouac. I made friends with Star the Shetland pony who appeared at once to be one of the more amiable and better-natured examples of his breed, and after satisfying his initial curiosity as to who this stranger was in his park, cantered off to lazily munch at the grass and watch my performance from the bottom of the field.

It was then that I discovered my second mistake. Always practise putting up a new tent before you set off camping, and particularly so if it is of a type and construction with which you are completely unfamiliar. I had at least the excuse of only buying the bivouac the day before I set out on the walk, but I should have known better and familiarized myself with it earlier that evening instead of supping beer in the pub.

Confusing and badly printed instructions; a style of tent which I had never come across before; and not least of all, numerous pints of Youngers Tartan Special, all combined to provide the locals of the Inver Arms with some of the best live Saturday night entertainment they had seen for some time as I struggled with that damn bivouac. At one point in the proceedings I pitched the whole lot into a heap in a fit of exasperated rage, and was reaching into my pocket for a box of matches determined that if nothing else I would at least have the satisfaction of burning the accursed thing and trust myself to bed and breakfast.

. . . confusing instructions . . . numerous pints . . . combined to provide best live Saturday night entertainment . . .

However, I calmed down and sobered up, and eventually the bivouac was erected. Well, probably not in the fashion which the manufacturers had intended, but sufficiently so for me to be able to crawl into my sleeping bag under cover and instantly fall asleep.

Awakening the next morning I was mildly surprised to find my shelter still upright. Dark clouds were rolling in menacingly from the west, so I hurriedly struck down the bivouac and packed my gear, not wanting to be caught unprepared in the rain. I had a hurried breakfast of Lucozade and Kendal mint cake, giving a piece of the mint cake to Star the pony who afterwards followed me to the end of the field with a look of utter devotion in his sleepy brown eyes.

Happily the threatening rain did not materialize as I pushed on south through steeply wooded Berriedale and onto the grim Ord of Caithness. Here the road curves in a U-bend, hemmed in by hills on one side and with a 750 foot drop to the sea on the other. On the grass of the cliff top at the northern end of the Ord is a macabre reminder of this road's dangers. In the clear cut brown earth scars bisect the green grass where a lorry misjudged the corner and plunged into the sea below, some time ago.

There is a superstition in Caithness concerning the Ord. If you are a Sinclair or a member of one of the many septs of the clan, it is regarded as extremely unlucky to cross the Ord on a Monday wearing the colour green. This superstition dates back to the year 1513 when William Sinclair, Earl of Caithness and chief of the clan, led a large party of men south, all clad in green, to the ill-fated battle of Flodden. A mere handful made the return journey to their home county. I noticed that I was wearing a green waterproof jacket, but then it was a Sunday and I am not a Sinclair, or superstitious . . . touch wood.

Around about midday I stopped for a rest at the picturesque little fishing village of Helmsdale where the river of the same name flows into the sea out of the Strath of Kildonan. The strath is famed for the Scottish gold rush, and equally infamous for the clearances of the crofters in favour of the more profitable and less troublesome sheep.

Years ago my brother had played football for Bunhildh Thistle, the football team which represented Helmsdale and played in the semi-professional Highland Reserve League. I remember him coming into the house and saying casually: "Well that's it. I've hit the big time now, signed forms with Bunhildh." "Semi-professional, eh?" I replied. "Much money in it?" . . . "Oh, they buy you a pair of boots each season, and you get a free meal at each away game."

Before I had set out on my journey I had bought in Thurso a small transistor radio. This cheap, battery-powered receiver frequently helped to make the day's walk more lightsome. I found that it fitted perfectly into one of the side bags on my backpack, and caused more than one look of surprise from a passer-by, as it appeared that I was carrying a singing and speaking backpack. Reception varied greatly from one part of the country to the next. I liked to tune into the local radio station whenever possible, as I found that the local weather reports were usually far more reliable than those given on the national network. As an example of the vagaries of reception, on this north-east leg, the Helmsdale area was the only area where I managed to obtain decent reception of the local station Moray Firth Radio.

Leaving Helmsdale I carried on south intending to stop for the night in Brora. Near the Wolf Stone, a memorial which commemorates the shooting of the last wolf in Scotland at a spot nearby, I met a fellow walker heading in the opposite direction to me. We stopped and chatted briefly but for the life of me I cannot remember his name. He told me that he was on his way to John O'Groats from Lands End, and I recall thinking slightly enviously at the time, that here was this chap almost finished his marathon walk, and there was me, barely started. Finally we parted company with me striding out confidently down the road, determined to conceal the slight limp which the blisters on my right foot were causing me, while under the scrutiny of this professional.

The early morning threat of rain finally came good as I was walking past the site of Kintradwell Broch, an Iron Age fortification in which were discovered two decapitated skeletons during excavations in the late 1800s. The rain steadily became heavier and heavier as I entered the outskirts of Brora.

Brora is noted for its beautiful golden sanded beaches, golf course and for once having the most northerly coal mine in Britain. The way the rain was beginning to pelt down, I would have willingly forsaken the delights of the first two for the shelter of the latter. However, I was very soon settled comfortably in the beautiful house belonging to James Simpson's cousin Rena and her husband. Rena had kindly offered me their hospitality when she had been on a weekend visit to Stroma earlier that year and I had told her about my plans for the walk. As the rain increased even further in intensity outside, I was more than glad to have a roof over my head in preference to my bivouac which was as yet untried in the rain.

After a good night's sleep and a massive breakfast, I disconsolately set off the following morning. Disconsolately because the previous evening I had witnessed Scotland suffer their second defeat of the World Cup, this time at the hands of the West Germans. To cheer me up though, the heavy rain had cleared and the sun was shining brightly. Low flying jets from RAF Lossiemouth streaked silver-grey in the blue, almost cloudless, sky.

Soon I was passing Dunrobin Castle, the ancient seat of the Dukes of Sutherland. High up above me on the summit of Beinn A' Bragaidh, the massive statue of the first Duke glowered down upon the town of Golspie and the ancestors of the people that his family did not consider as important as sheep.

Pushing on through Golspie I could see clear across the Dornoch Firth to the tower of the now automatic lighthouse at Tarbet Ness. It was at about this spot where the famous Highland clairvoyant, the Brahn Seer helped to provide one of the earliest if briefest one-man lighthouses. This was where he was burned alive in a tar barrel on the orders of the Duchess of Seaforth. A statutory lesson in the perils of telling a woman the truth about her husband.

The traffic was fairly light but I had one hairy moment when crossing the causeway built by Thomas Telford over Loch Fleet and was forced to back up well off the road as a line of articulated lorries thundered past.

I briefly thought of stopping and camping for the night among the oak and birch groves on the outskirts of Spinningdale where the late James Robertson Justice used to live. But finally I halted for the day just outside of Bonar Bridge, the bridge being yet another Telford construction. I had a little trouble erecting the bivouac, but anyway, the night was so beautiful I think that I could have willingly played at cowboys and slept under the stars. I was certainly tired enough to do so.

Rather than walk the long way around the coast via the towns of Tain and Alness, I took the shorter and far more picturesque route across the hill of Struie. The Ross-shire countryside spread all around me in a beautiful panorama:.barren grey rocks dotted with dull green lichen, ages old, sedge and ochre-coloured moorland, chocolate brown peat bogs, patches of shiny green bracken and yellow gorse, and the glistening silver and white of swift running shallow burns. Black faced sheep, 'brockies', played 'chicken' on the road with the cars of frustrated tourists.

After an easy and pleasant day's walk I arrived in Evanton, on the shores of the Cromarty Firth. The weather was steadily beginning to look distinctly menacing, so I decided to opt for bed and breakfast that night at one of the town's hotels. The small town of Evanton was unconsciously responsible for providing a certain well-known English football club with one of its staunchest supporters. This all happened when my brother and I were both young boys and my father had taken the car and was driving the family down south for a holiday in England. We passed through Evanton on the road to Inverness, and my brother, who would be about six years old at the time, on seeing the name of the place, declared that this must be where the famous football team came from. Puzzled, we quizzed him as to which team did he mean, and to our amusement we discovered that he had confused the name with that of the famous Liverpool-based team of Everton. We patiently explained his mistake, pointing out to him quite reasonably, what would a small Ross-shire village be doing with a football team in the English first division. But he would not be swayed, and declared that from now on that was the team which he was going to support. He's in his thirties now and still an 'Evanton' supporter.

I relaxed that night over a couple of pints in one of the local pubs, and listened to several conflicting and highly improbable stories about the cricketer Ian Botham who had tarried here on his recent John O'Groats to Lands End walk.

At breakfast the following morning I chatted to two travelling salesmen, the only other residents at the hotel. In the course of the conversation one of the reps told me that he had been listening to Radio Scotland and had heard the morning's weather report, and the outlook was pretty bleak for the next twenty-four hours.

Well things started out just fine. I paid my bill and headed off for the new Cromarty Firth road bridge which loomed up in the distance. Radio Scotland's morning show blared out of the transistor in the side pocket of my backpack, to help jolly me along. I think that was the only time I was jolly on that particular day's walk.

Once across the road bridge and onto the Black Isle it began to spit ominously with rain, and at the same time, the wind began to freshen. In less than fifteen minutes the conditions had deteriorated to a torrential downpour backed by a howling northerly gale which felt as if it was blowing clear off the polar ice cap. For the next twelve miles or so to Inverness there was literally no shelter whatsoever, and I was forced to push on and bear it. I do not think that I have been wetter or more miserable in my life. The really heavy rain had started so suddenly and with such violence that I had no time to put on my waterproof leggings, and in consequence my track suit trousers were soon clammily sticking to my legs as I grimly plodded on. All around me the Black Isle countryside had been reduced to a misty, grey-green washed out blur. After a time my boots began to leak and squelching socks helped to add to the general misery and discomfort. I was walking against the traffic on a dual carriageway and every so often a large lorry or bus would go roaring past, casting up a bow wave of water and saturating spray which would drench me even further. It came to a point that I was so cold, wet and miserable that I just did not let it bother me any more. My brain switched to automatic pilot and I merely plodded on, head down following the roadside, the goal of reaching Inverness and shelter the most important thing in the entire world.

Although weeks later I was to have some bad days of weather when walking up the west coast of Scotland, I do believe that twelve mile traverse of the Black Isle was the worst of the entire journey. When I finally arrived at Kessock and the approaches to the bridge leading into Inverness which I could dimly see through the driving greyness on the opposite bank of the Beauly Firth, I could have almost cried with joy and relief.

My first stop in 'the capital of the Highlands', was the nearest pub where I ordered a stiff double rum to help fortify my spirit against the freezing cold and wetness I had just endured. Standing at the bar, I glanced down and noticed the ever-widening pool of water at my feet caused as the moisture streamed off my sodden clothes and seeped out of my boots. The elderly barman looked at my dishevelled state, then slowly he looked down at the pool on the floor. "A bitty damp outside is it?" he enquired politely.

An old friend of mine, Ian Milne, and his wife Margaret, had said that they would be pleased to put me up for the night in Inverness. It was sheer heaven to lie back and have a good soak in a hot bath at their lovely new house. After a change into dry clothes, a hot meal, and another stiff rum, I had almost completely forgotten the miserable discomfort of most of that day. However, I had some very wet clothing and boots to remind me, and it was obvious that I would have to take a day off in Inverness while I dried everything out thoroughly, especially the boots.

I was not the only one to have suffered from the elements that day. Although it was barely two weeks from the summer solstice, there were reports on the evening news of blizzards in the Braemar area and two

. . . so cold, wet and miserable . . .

highland roads had been temporarily blocked with snow. There were also accounts of swollen rivers and flooding in some low lying areas. As I said before — flaming June!

With both Margaret and Ian away at their work in the morning, I had a leisurely lie in before bundling my clothing together and heading up into the town centre in search of a laundromat and also with the intention of doing a little shopping. It is recorded that it was in or near Inverness where Bridei, or Brude, King of the Picts, had his capital in ancient days. The enigmatic Picts have long intrigued me as they have left many memorials to their passing in Caithness. In fact there is a chambered cairn burial mound not a hundred yards from the lighthouse on Stroma. The waters which swirl past the lighthouse are named after them, Pentland Firth merely being an alternative of Pictland Firth. The 'Caith' part in the name Caithness is reputed to be a corruption of 'Catti' the name of the local Pictish tribe.

The early Picts had some interesting social habits, such as head hunting, cannibalism, tattooing, and fornicating in public. My only comment is that old King Brude's Inverness must have been a sight more livelier than it is today.

With the odds and ends of my shopping done, and my clothing happily tumbling in the laundromat's tumble drier, I decided to amuse myself for the afternoon by paying a visit to the local Ladbrokes the bookmakers. In a recent promotion by Scottish and Newcastle breweries, I had managed to accumulate twenty pounds worth of free Ladbroke betting vouchers. As there is no Ladbroke bookmakers in either Thurso or Wick, I had brought these free bets with me with the intention of trying my luck here and there, and possibly boosting my slender funds. After all, if I lost it was not coming out of my pocket.

I have been fond of the 'sport of kings' since I was a boy and the day when I managed to persuade my father to put half-a-crown for me on a horse called Team Spirit in the 1964 Grand National. Team Spirit duly won, and incidentally to date has been the last winner of that particular race I have backed. A couple of years ago I had an Injured Jockeys' Fund calendar on the wall of my living room. On being asked by one of my friends why I supported such a charity, I replied that it was because I felt so guilty that so many jockeys were injured falling off horses which I had backed.

As things turned out though, that afternoon was quite profitable. The only loss I sustained was two pounds worth of betting vouchers, when in a moment of badness, I backed Poland to defeat England in that evening's World Cup tie. England won three – nil.

The East Coast...

Sunburn and more World Cup

 KITTED out in dry, clean clothes with dry, freshly dubbin'd boots on my feet, and Doctor Scholl's moleskin protecting my tender blisters, I bid goodbye to Ian Milne outside of Inverness Technical College where he teaches, and left Inverness, heading east. My main preoccupation for the first couple of miles of that day's walk, was in keeping a wary eye on the heavy, early morning traffic, as I was now walking beside the main road to Aberdeen.

Just to the south of me was situated Drumossie Moor, the site of the tragic and bloody battle of Culloden on 16th April, 1746. This was the last pitched battle fought on British soil and the innocent originator of more historically-twisted bullshit than you can shake a big stick at. What is so tragically true though is that it was on this bleak stretch of moorland where the Hanoverian artillery under the command of Colonel Belford wreaked such deadly carnage amongst the massed ranks of the Jacobite army; and it was here where the redcoats of Barrel and Munro's regiments stoutly repulsed the last desperate charge of the rebel Highlanders. This was the place where the Stuart cause was irretrievably lost, and the confused and bewildered Prince Charles Edward Stuart was led from the battlefield in tears with the taunting cries of Lord Elcho, commander of the lifeguards, ringing in his ears: "Run you cowardly Italian! Run!"

My thoughts turned from that far-off battle to the more immediate problems of keeping an eye on the approaching traffic. The weather was fairly indifferent, and apart from the occasional patch of forest, so was the countryside. I tried to break the monotony by listening to Radio Scotland on my radio, but the roar of the passing cars, lorries and buses, drowned out most of what was being said.

On reaching the town of Nairn I decided to stop for something to eat and drink in the shape of a couple of delicious bridies from one of the local bakers, washed down with a pint of milk. Harking back to Culloden again, it was in Nairn where the Hanoverian Army camped the night before the battle. The redcoats had drunk the health of their commander, William Augustus, Duke of Cumberland, with loud toasts of 'Billy and Flanders!' It was Cumberland's birthday and he had provided brandy for the men out of his own pocket.

Leaving Nairn behind me I pushed on to nearby Brodie castle where I had intended camping for the night. On my arrival at the village, I discovered that the campsite marked on my map no longer existed. I chatted to one of the locals and he told me that there was an excellent campsite at the village of Mundole, a few miles down the road, on the outskirts of Forres. Although I felt little inclination to travel further that day, I also had little option, and so I wearily plodded on, arriving at the campsite about eight o'clock that evening.

I must admit that when I arrived at Mundole I thought the extra miles well worth it. The campsite was situated in a large, level field sheltered by stands of trees. A small river bordered one side of the site, in which a couple of young boys were fishing hopefully. Because it was still early in the season, the site was almost deserted apart from a couple of residential caravans, and I could more or less pick my spot. I had the bivouac erected in next to no time — I was becoming quite proficient with it by now — and I took off to a nearby pub called the Elizabethan Arms, the proximity of which I considered another plus on the merits of the Mundole campsite. I discovered in the pub that I was the only customer and I enjoyed a couple of pints and a pleasant chat with the owners Mr. and Mrs. Mackay.

Awakening in the morning I unzipped the entrance to the bivouac and cautiously stuck my head out to find a bright yellow sun shining in a cloudless, blue sky. A faint mist was drifting lazily off the river where martins were flying hither and thither, hawking for flies. It seemed that summer had finally arrived.

I leisurely dismantled and packed the bivouac, and then shouldering my backpack I set off to see if I could find the campsite proprietor and square up for the night. This proved a fruitless search so I strode off to the main road where I enjoyed a hearty breakfast in a Little Chef cafe before walking half a mile or so into Forres.

The town of Forres, which at one time nobody with the surname Innes was allowed to enter due to a clause in a treaty between the feuding clans of Innes and Dunbar, was just wakening up. Shops were beginning to open, the enticing aroma of fresh bread drifted from the open doorway of a baker's shop as I passed and wove my way through throngs of neatly dressed, freshly scrubbed, schoolchildren making their way to school. This peaceful scene was suddenly shattered by the earsplitting roar of two fighter jet aircraft from RAF Lossiemouth which came screaming over the town nearly at rooftop level. The citizens of Forres must be well inured to such visits as I only noticed one other person as well as myself, stop and gaze up at the passing aircraft. He must have been an Innes.

I left Forres, branching off the main Aberdeen road and heading north towards the coast. A short distance out of the town, the road ran alongside the sprawling airbase of RAF Kinloss. When I was a boy, I had for a time been a member of Thurso's Air Training Corps — I think it must have broken the CO's heart when he found out that it was the Royal Navy I had left to join — and we spent many happy camps here at Kinloss. We cadets would be taken up in Shackletons for flights over the North Sea, and occasionally he allowed a shot of the controls in a Chipmunk trainer aircraft. We would spend our evenings drinking under age in the nearby Abbey pub, hoping that our cadet uniforms would fool the barman into thinking that we were seasoned, regular aircraftsmen on our night off. I was shaken out of these nostalgic memories as a huge, predatory shadow suddenly passed over me, and I looked up to see the light grey underbelly of a Nimrod aircraft coming in to land.

Once past the airbase, I walked on through flat farmlands. The road was hemmed in with high hedgerows on either side of me, and the traffic was agreeably light. My transistor radio was blaring out pop music, this was Radio One reception country. I noticed that some pop records had an excellent beat for hiking to. The number one record at that time, 'Doctor and the Medics' with the re-release of "Spirit in the Sky" was one record particularly suited for this. So was Robert Palmer's "Addicted to Love", although the mental picture of his glamorous, all female, backing group might have helped inspire me with that one.

The day steadily became hotter and hotter, and I was quite grateful to enter the shade and comparative coolness of the pine woods of Roseisle Forest. A busload of children passed, and the five little horrors in the back seat made various gestures and grimaces at me through the back window. I favoured them with one of my better snarls.

At Burghead I looked down once more upon the Moray Firth. There was a haze on the still waters which made an RAF launch, lying close inshore, appear to be suspended over the surface of the sea, the grey of the launch's hull merging and blurring into the misty blue background. Burghead was once an important grain shipping port, but now relies mainly upon tourism and fishing. It is a pretty little town, particularly in favourable weather as when I visited the place.

I pushed on eastwards, passing through the sleepy village of Cummingstown and on into neighbouring Hopeman. By this time I was feeling pretty dehydrated from walking in the still heat of the day, and arriving in Hopeman I decided to pop into a pub called 'The Neuk' for a cool pint of beer. The pub was owned by an Englishman called Mick, who proved to be an excellent host. When he found out that I was on a sponsored walk for the lifeboat service, he immediately demanded a sponsor form from me and began to badger his local customers. The majority of the pub's patrons being fishermen, they did not need much badgering. I found that I knew one or two of the clientele from occasions in the past when their boats had put in at Scrabster.

It took a great effort of will to leave that friendly little pub and the excellent session which was beginning to develop between myself, Mick, and the crews of the fishing boats 'Harmony' and 'Sharona', but I had the presence of mind to get out while I could still walk, and with shouts of "Be sure to come down to the boats and see us if we are in Kinlochbervie when you eventually arrive there!" echoing behind me, I headed off down the road once more.

Thankfully there was only a handful of miles to my next stop at Covesea Skerries lighthouse on the outskirts of Lossiemouth. I was doubly grateful that I did not have far to go, as the afternoon heat was becoming murderous. Passing traffic kicked up plumes of gritty dust as it drove by, and the thought of a bath at Covesea helped to spur me on.

It could possibly be argued that Covesea Skerries was the site of what may have been the first lighthouse in Scotland. Legend has it that in the ninth century, it was at this spot that the monk St. Gerardine used to stand on the foreshore with a lantern to guide passing ships past the dangerous off-shore skerries, which are today named in memory of him as the Halliman (Holyman) skerries. The saint is depicted in the coat of arms of Lossiemouth, clutching a lantern in his hand which he is displaying to a passing ship.

Covesea lighthouse
courtesy Northern
Lighthouse Board

The present lighthouse was built in 1864. Twenty years after it was first proposed a disastrous storm sunk sixteen vessels in the Moray Firth.

Nowadays, Covesea Skerries is a fully automatic lighthouse, but I had been requested to call there as the lighthouse station was now used as a holiday home for Northern Lighthouse Board personnel and their families. I must confess that I had been of the opinion that as I lived at one lighthouse, and worked at another, this particular type of establishment would have been the very last place I would have chosen to spend my holidays, but I admit I was pleasantly surprised by what I saw. Surrounded by clumps of yellow flowering gorse, and fronted by clean, sandy beaches, it is a picturesque little spot. The rooms were clean, tidy and well-maintained, and provided with a colour television in each of the ex-accommodation houses where the visiting families stay. From the lighthouse courtyard you get an excellent view of Branderburgh and Lossiemouth, and in particular you can look almost directly down upon RAF Lossiemouth which can provide hours of cheap entertainment, if you don't mind the noise, watching the jets taking off and landing.

Staying at Covesea that week were Duncan Macpherson, his wife and young son. Duncan was an old friend of mine. He had come to the job at about the same time as me and we had both been stationed together at Hyskeir lighthouse when we were still Supernumary lightkeepers. Supernumary was the title given to a trainee lightkeeper who had not yet been appointed as a full-time lightkeeper at any specific lighthouse but was moved around from lighthouse to lighthouse, either for training purposes or to relieve one of the resident lightkeepers who had to go off duty due to illness, etc. The old term for Supernumary lightkeeper used to be 'Expectant lightkeeper'; a quaint old-fashioned piece of terminology which has never failed to tickle my own particular twisted sense of humour.

That evening the Macpherson family had decided to go off for a drive into Elgin leaving me with the place to myself. First I enjoyed the promised luxury of a warm bath, and then with a pie and chip supper and four tins of McEwans export beer, I settled down in front of the television to watch the crucial Scotland versus Uruguay World Cup tie, which resulted in a goalless draw, Scotland's elimination from the World Cup and my wondering if it was too late in life to become a rugby fan.

After bidding goodbye, I set off the next morning in good heart despite the football result. Duncan and his wife were leaving later that day, returning to Duncan's native island of Skye where he was assistant lightkeeper at Neist Point lighthouse. I seemed to spend hours walking around the perimeter of RAF Lossiemouth. I thought back to the last time I had been hereabouts, back in the early 1970s when the place had been called HMS Fulmar and had been the Fleet Air Arm base for the Buccaneer

... 'Expectant lightkeeper'; a quaint ... terminology ...

jets used by the navy. I had been a very junior radio operator on the aircraft carrier HMS Ark Royal at the time. What I remember chiefly about the weekend we visited Lossiemouth was that the national census was being carried out, and some bright spark unwittingly boosted the population of Scotland by over two thousand by giving everyone on the Ark Royal a Scottish census form. I remember grinning at an overheard conversation between two Cockneys in my messdeck, who were busily filling in the form: "'Ere Wiggy, can I speak Garlic?"

Once RAF Lossiemouth was behind me, I spent the rest of that forenoon following the peaceful back road which meandered through patches of wooded country and rich farmlands, and enabled me to bypass Elgin before I rejoined the main Aberdeen to Inverness road, a few miles before Fochabers.

The tranquillity of the morning was quickly forgotten as I joined up with the main stream of traffic once more. The day had by now become roasting hot, and on the road to Fochabers the traffic was non-stop. There was very little wind and the stench of exhaust fumes was so bad that when I stopped to smoke a roll-up, it almost felt a healthy past-time.

I arrived in Fochabers feeling hot, sweaty, and extremely thirsty. The time was around half past three in the afternoon, and I praised Scotland's enlightened licensing laws as I stumbled into the Gordon Arms to replace lost body moisture. My chief memories of the little town of Fochabers was of the numerous shops selling tweed and tartans to predominantly elderly tourists. On my way out of town I passed Baxter's food factory, and judging by the number of cars parked outside in the car park, it was proving to be a favourite stopping off place for visitors.

I managed to leave the main road once again at Fochabers which allowed me to enjoy a couple of miles of sun-dappled shade as I passed through woodlands where Scots pines and birch trees seemed in predominance. Dotted between the trees and along the verge of the road were large clumps of purple foxgloves with here and there the occasional less common white variety. If I was to be asked which flower did I notice the most throughout the entire walk, my reply would have to be the foxglove. It seems to be ubiquitous in Scotland nowadays. I walked past them on the rough heath and moorland of Sutherland, and I saw clumps of them interspersed with the brambles, burnet roses and dog roses of the Galloway hedgerows.

It had been my original intention that day to head for Cullen, where there was a campsite marked on my map. However, the road I was walking along just bypassed Buckie, and on the spur of the moment, I abruptly altered my plans and turned off to enter the town in the hope that I might find somewhere to spend the night there. This turned out to be one of my better decisions.

Wandering into Buckie I went into the Commercial bar for a pint of beer and to enquire of the locals if there was a Fisherman's Mission in the town where I might get a bath and possibly a bed for the night. The very first person I spoke to informed me that surprisingly enough for such a renowned Scottish fishing port, there was no Fisherman's Mission in the town. Then when he noticed my backpack and general attire, he asked me that if by any chance was I the lightkeeper who was doing the sponsored walk for the RNLI?

Slightly surprised at the recognition, I replied that I was he. With a broad grin on his face, the man warmly shook my hand and introduced himself as Barry Anderson, owner of the Northern Light bar and secretary of the local lifeboat committee.

"We were warned to look out for you," he said. "You can stay at my place tonight. Now, let's get some of these sponsor forms around the local pubs!"

I stayed at Barry's house that night, and here I came across one of the many experiences that I was to have throughout the entire journey, which brought home to me the fact as to just what a small nation Scotland is. I began to call this kind of experience the 'Jock Tamson syndrome'.

Barry had a small kitten which was playing on the living room carpet when we entered his house. I commented on the animal, and he replied that he had just acquired the cat the previous weekend when he had been on holiday up north with his children. He said that the cat had been given to him by the woman who owns the Farr Bay Inn near Bettyhill in north Sutherland. Now it just so happened that the weekend before I had set out on my walk, I had been in that very same pub, and offered the very same cat by the very same woman.

I arose the next morning with the unmistakable symptoms of a hangover. The day's scorching heat did little to help matters, and I did not so much as walk out of Buckie, but rather slunk.

However every cloud has a silver lining, or in this case, the lack of clouds, as the heat helped to sweat the alcohol out of my system, and a bottle of Barrs Irn Bru off the cold shelf of a newsagents shop in Cullen helped to restore me to almost perfect health again. Cullen is a fine example of what the power of money could do in the last century. The fine town square and main street were built in 1823 by the earl of Seafield and Findlater, in order to move the old town of Cullen a further half mile away from his own private house.

By early afternoon I had arrived at the picture postcard seaside town of Portsoy. Tempted by a menu displayed outside one of the local hotels, I wandered into the lounge bar and enjoyed a very tasty bar lunch of fresh, fried haddock and chips. I must admit I felt a little bit self-conscious and downright scruffy, dressed in my hiking gear of tattered tracksuit trousers and sweat-stained T-shirt. The rest of the customers seemed to be mainly couples and families dressed in their best summer clothes and out for a Sunday dinner treat.

With Jimmy Savile prattling away on the transistor radio, I left Portsoy and headed along the coast road for Banff. It was hot and dusty, a yellow-white sun burned fiercely in a blazing blue sky, and I found myself subconsciously whistling the 'Legion's last patrol'.

I recalled having read in a brochure that Banff was once a very fashionable resort, and judging by the throngs of people about the place when I arrived there, this seaside town has not yet gone out of fashion, at least not with the people of the north-east. The sandy beach was packed with sun worshippers. There were men wearing shorts and a vast variety of T-shirts, women looking pretty and peeling in halter-backs and sunglasses, while small children with ice-cream moustaches, scuttled about naturally bare-bummed, clutching shovels and pails. There was a holiday atmosphere about the place, but I had personally had quite enough of the sun for one day and I headed for the nearest shady bar and a cool pint of beer.

I watched the latest World Cup action on the television in the bar, but it was interrupted viewing. I had been given the 'phone number of a friend

... bare-bummed, clutching shovels and pails ...

of my brother's who lived in Banff, who had said he would be willing to put me up for the night should I stop off in the town. He must have been away for the weekend because after numerous unsuccessful attempts to 'phone him I finally gave it up as a bad job and decided to find somewhere to camp for the night. My map indicated that there was a campsite on the outskirts of the town, and finishing my beer I set off to find it. A short distance from the bar I found a signpost indicating the way to the campsite, but no mileage. After I had followed this road for half a mile or so, I stopped a passer-by and asked him for directions. To my annoyance he told me that the site was another four miles at least along the road, and he believed that only caravans were permitted there. However, he told me that there was another campsite situated about a mile or so out of Macduff, Banff's neighbouring town.

Retracing my steps I returned to Banff and crossed the bridge over the river Deveron which separates Banff from Macduff. This elegant seven arch bridge has a connection with lighthouses, as it was designed by John Smeaton, the man who was the architect for the third Eddystone lighthouse.

After a walk of about twenty minutes I spotted the campsite in a field next to a farm about a hundred yards off the main road. I called on the owner of the site, the local farmer, and I asked him for permission to put up my bivouac for the night. When I told him about my walk, he was more than willing to forego the charge for the night's camping, telling me that only the previous week he had allowed a party of Royal Marines who had been on a sponsored walk, to camp in his field. In the half-light I speedily erected the bivouac, crawled in, and was almost immediately asleep.

A welcome, cool breeze greeted me as I poked my head out of the bivouac the following morning. The sky still remained blue and cloudless but this fresh draught off the sea helped to take a lot of heat out of the morning. I was grateful for this because after the roasting hot weather of the past few days, my arms had become quite badly sunburned and I found it extremely painful hoisting my pack onto my back, as the shoulder straps chafed the red, blistered skin.

Consulting my map I saw that there was a choice of two roads which I could follow to arrive at my planned destination for that day, which was to be Kinnaird Head lighthouse at Fraserburgh. I could choose the main road or a secondary coastal route. As far as I could judge, the coastal route seemed to be at least a good two miles shorter, and would have the decided advantage of being used by less traffic, so this was the route I decided upon. It is only a pity that I did not take more notice of the little chevron signs on the road map which denoted steep hills.

The route was certainly scenic enough with the deep blue of the Moray Firth contrasting beautifully with the bright yellow of the gorse and furze. Campions, poppies, cranesbill and the ever-present foxgloves, brightened up the grassy verges at the side of the road; and the traffic was almost non-existent. But the road itself dipped and rose like a demented roller-coaster. Over the course of this road I encountered some of the steepest hills of the entire journey. One particularly memorable hill was at a place called Pennan, a small village made famous by the filming on location there of parts of the movie 'Local Hero'. After I had wearily negotiated this particular back-breaker of a gradient, I was almost on my knees. I sat back to rest for a good fifteen minutes, propped up by my backpack as I vacantly watched the ever-present Lossiemouth jets playing tag over Rosehearty.

Shortly after midday I arrived at the village of New Aberdour. The place was like a ghost town, with shops shut and not a soul stirring on the neatly laid out parallel streets. At the local Commercial Hotel I discovered that today was the town's public holiday and almost everyone would have gone to Fraserburgh for the day. I had a couple of pints and a friendly chat with John the pub landlord, an ex-fisherman who had recently retired and bought the Commercial. The general conversation came around to the topic of my walk, and I found that he was of much the same opinion as me on one aspect of it — that while the RNLI deserves all our support, it is a bit shameful that a country like Britain which has made so much of its past wealth from the sea, should have to rely on charity for its lifeboat service It should long ago have set up a government financed organization, something alone the lines of the coastguard.

Leaving the slightly eery and deserted town of New Aberdour behind me, I pushed on through the fertile Buchan farmland, noting the sleek, healthy-looking cattle in the fields as I passed by. The reaction of cattle grazing in a field as I was passing, never failed to amuse me. Invariably one of the beasts would pop its head up from the grass, and on spotting me would turn to its fellows as if to say: "Hey, waddya know, here's an idiot of a hiker! Let's all go over and have a good look at the clown!" Then the entire herd would come belting across the field to join me on their side of the hedge or fence and follow me until the end of the field, jostling and bumping each other as if in an effort to get a better view of this distraction.

... here's an idiot of a hiker! ...

I rejoined the main road at Mid Ardlaw, and in an hour or so I was walking into the outskirts of Fraserburgh, the thriving east coast fishing port which was founded back in the 16th century by earl Fraser of Philorth.

Kinnaird Head lighthouse is situated in the town itself, directly on the coast where it looks down upon the busy harbour. This lighthouse has the distinction of being the very first lighthouse to be established by the Northern Lighthouse Board back in 1787. To give you some idea of just how long ago that was, King George III was on the throne, and it was only four years since the end of the American War of Independence. The light was situated on top of a small coastal castle which was built by Alexander Fraser in 1570, and apart from obvious technological alterations over the years, that is where it still is. Probably one of the oddest and oldest light-towers in the country.

On my arrival I introduced myself to Alec Mowat the principal lightkeeper, whom I had never met before, but over a cup of tea discovered that we had several acquaintances in common. I was to stay overnight at Kinnaird in the bothy which is kept for the use of visiting relief keepers, and sometimes used by the Local or Occasional lightkeeper. These are lightkeepers who live locally and are either employed full or part-time at the lighthouse. I stayed in quite a few lighthouse bothies during the course of my journey, and I remember commenting at one of them, that

Kinnaird Head lighthouse
courtesy Northern Lighthouse Board

when I had finished my walk I could write the equivalent of an AA or RAC hotel guide, entitled the 'Cassells guide to lighthouse bothies'. Kinnaird Head's bothy was certainly worthy of a five star rating, one of the best I was to stay in.

Having never been to Fraserburgh before, I took a wander around the town that evening, returning early to the lighthouse to 'phone my parents and daughter. The day before I had set out on my walk I had given my daughter a large map of Scotland, and said I would 'phone home whenever possible to inform her of my whereabouts which she was diligently plotting with coloured pins.

Although I was eager to be off the next day, my start was delayed due to a representative of the local press. This manifested itself in the form of a very charming lady photographer, whose name escapes me completely. This lady took her job very seriously, and must have gone through several reels of film that morning. She had me pose with Mrs. Mowat and her daughter, by myself, next to the light-tower, next to the accommodation building, next to the main gate . . . with my backpack on, with my backpack off . . . down on the foreshore looking heroically out to sea . . . and finally in various poses with principal keeper Alec Mowat who had put on his best uniform suit for the occasion.

In fact it was Alec's patience which snapped first. The lady photographer asked the two of us to shake hands for her picture, to make it appear that I had just arrived and Alec was greeting me. "Lovely" she said, once we were in position. "Now look into his eyes," she instructed Alec, who quickly spun round on his heel and indignantly snorted that he was not a "damn poofter!"

Thankfully I later discovered that as press photographers went, this lady was an exception to the rule. I found that the majority of them were quite content to take a quick couple of snaps before disappearing into the nearest pub.

It was to be quite a nerve-racking morning's walk when I eventually managed to clear the town. The road south out of Fraserburgh twisted and turned around blind, tree-screened corners, and seemed to me to have a disproportionately large number of heavy lorries thundering along it. Matters took a severe turn for the worse when after about a mile a clammy, grey haar drifted in off the North Sea and reduced visibility to about twenty yards. However, I noticed that it did not reduce the speed of the traffic. It was a hair-raising time but things had improved by the time I reached Crimond, and the traffic had become a lot lighter and so had the visibility with the mist having drifted back out to sea. Looking up I noticed that the sky overhead had taken on a pale grey colour, tinged with yellow ochre. The air felt heavy and oppressive, and I felt distinctly uneasy. A feeling which I put down at the time to nervous exhaustion after walking against heavy traffic in such poor visibility.

I passed a signpost indicating the turn off for the road to Rattray. This is where the lighthouse of Rattray Head is situated, lying just off the sand-dune dotted coast. I spent the Christmas and New Year of 1979 at this lighthouse which was fully manned in those days but is now completely automatic. It was while I was here that I first received news that my daughter was expected. Rattray Head lighthouse used to have an interesting and unusual relief system. Although the lighthouse was situated off-shore, neither boat or helicopter was used to relieve the keepers or take out provisions, but instead a tractor and trailer used to drive out over the sands at low tide, making it probably the only place where the lighthouse boatman was actually the lighthouse tractorman.

The massive industrial complex of the St. Fergus oil and gas terminal loomed alongside of me as I steadily walked south. Tanks gleaming dully and a spaghetti junction of pipework behind a high, wire-mesh security fence. The radars at RAF Buchan began to play gyp with my reception of Radio Scotland on the backpack transistor, and the day was beginning to feel even more threatening and oppressive.

Peterhead was to be my destination for the day, and while I was walking past the Peterhead golf course, with the town in full view less than half a mile ahead, I discovered the reason behind the day's feeling of uneasiness. A bright yellow flash lit up the entire horizon from east to west in front of me, and after a short pause, was followed by the deep, rumbling growl of thunder.

For the first few minutes I kept on walking, quickening my pace as the rain had not arrived yet. But the pauses between the bright yellow flashes and the heavy rumbles was becoming shorter and shorter, and soon sporadic raindrops began to fall, leaving spots on the dry, dusty ground.

At that precise moment, a transit van pulled up alongside of me and the driver shouted out did I want a lift into town. My soaking in the Black Isle was still very fresh in my memory and I did not even stop to consider the offer but gratefully leaped into the vacant passenger seat just as the lightning flashes and thunder rolled concurrently and the rains began to sheet down.

It would not have annoyed me too much if I had received a complete and utter soaking at the start of the day's walk, or even for that matter, half way through. But the thought of getting a drenching when only a few hundred yards from my destination, was just not on. Sod the precise ethics of the situation, I am glad I took that lift. The driver of the transit introduced himself as Ross Macdonald, and said that he had read about me in the papers. He very kindly dropped me off at the door of the Palace Hotel from where I would be able to 'phone my host for the night, and enjoy a quick pint of beer.

My host for that night was to be Graham Milne — I seemed to do well with hospitality from the Milne clan — who was a teacher in Peterhead and a long distance running pal of my brother Stephen, who incidentally is also a teacher. Graham lived in the village of Longside, situated to the landward of Peterhead. He had told me to ring him up as soon as I hit the town, and he would come and pick me up. Longside has a connection with the Northern Lighthouse Board, because the Bolkow BO 105 helicopters belonging to Bond Helicopters, and which are chartered by the Board, are based at the airport here.

After a short wait of about twenty minutes, Graham arrived to take me to his house at Longside. That is after he had first downed two pints of beer in the time it took me to drink half a pint. This last feat did not surprise me as it is a peculiarity which I have observed in several marathon runners before — and teachers!

Graham's wife Wilma had a very tasty meal prepared for us when we arrived, which I tackled with gusto. That evening it was pure luxury to sit in the Milne's living room after a long, slow, hot bath, watching the latest World Cup football game of France versus Italy, while the thunder and lightning outside evoked a mental picture of the 'twilight of the gods'.

I slept soundly that night as the foul weather without continued to rage. Happily it was to prove short-lived and in the morning I awoke to find that the thunderstorms had moved out over the North Sea, and the day held a promise of becoming quite pleasant. After a filling breakfast with the Milne family, Graham gave me a lift back into Peterhead where I intended resuming my trek.

Peterhead was once one of Britain's premier whaling ports, but now, mainly due to cheaper landing fees than nearby Aberdeen, it is certainly one of Britain's premier fishing ports. Dozens of fish lorries tumbled past me as I headed out of town past the grim and notorious Peterhead prison, famous for the al fresco get-togethers its inmates occasionally hold on the roof.

A short walk brought me to the neighbouring village of Boddam where I was to call in at the lighthouse of Buchan Ness, a candy-striped light-tower situated on the rocky foreshore by the village.

Buchan Ness lighthouse
courtesy Christopher Nicholson

Built in 1827 by Aberdeen contractor John Gibb, Buchan Ness light-house is a one-man operated station now, soon to be fully automated. Principal lightkeeper John Malcolm was the man in charge and he ushered me in for a very welcome cup of tea or two while he signed my check sheet and I 'phoned headquarters to advise them of my whereabouts. I had served briefly with John some years ago at Dunnet Head lighthouse, but unfortunately I did not have the time to linger too long for a good chat as I was keen to push on that day, hoping to reach Newburgh by evening.

On John's advice I managed to avoid the heavy traffic on the main road by taking the quieter coastal route past the picturesque Bullers of Buchan and Slains castle. The original Slains castle was utterly destroyed after the owner, the earl of Erroll, who was head of the Catholic cause in the turbulent Scotland of the time, rashly threatened Aberdeen with 'fire and sword' in 1594. One hundred and fifty or so years later, the rebuilt and re-sited stronghold was being used as a clandestine entry port into the country for Jacobite agents who had come across from Europe.

I stopped briefly for a midday snack at the Kilmarnock Arms in Cruden Bay. The name Cruden Bay had been nagging at the back of my mind all that morning, and it was to be a field full of horses and ponies on the outskirts of the village which finally struck the chord of my memory. When I was living in Shetland I had owned a Welsh Cob mare, and it was from Cruden Bay that I had bought her, sight unseen, and shipped her up to Lerwick from Aberdeen. Cuckoo was her name, and she was a sweet old lady who stoically tolerated such an atrocious horseman as myself. I like to think that we had some good times together, because I certainly enjoyed the partnership.

The afternoon hike was fairly uneventful with the weather now bright and sunny once more, and the traffic light and comprising mainly tourists instead of heavy lorries. For the first time, Radio Aberdeen was coming through loud and clear on my backpack transistor. Funnily enough, due to the vagaries of radio transmission I received the best reception of Radio Aberdeen later on the walk when on the road to St. Abbs Head lighthouse down on the border.

In the early evening I crossed the bridge over the river Ythan and duly arrived at my planned destination of Newburgh. I walked through the town heading for the southern outskirts as it was to be a bivouac night tonight and I was hoping to find somewhere to camp, possibly by the beach. Just before the road led out of the town I passed the Ythan Hotel and noticed a sign displayed there advertising camping facilities. I entered the public bar to make enquiries about permission to camp, explaining to the landlord that I was on a sponsored walk for the RNLI, and that I only had a small bivouac tent, so would he agree to let me camp for free. He readily consented and gave me directions on how to get to the neighbouring field which he used as a campsite. Although it was nice and comfortable in the bar, I had learned my lesson at the Inver Arms in Dunbeath, so after downing a single pint of beer, I left to pitch my bivouac.

It was an excellent campsite on flat, sandy ground which held the tent pegs well. As soon as I had everything sorted out and ready for the night, I returned to the hotel bar and ordered a bar supper as I had had nohing to eat since a bag of crisps in the Kilmarnock Arms that lunch time. Taking a comfortable seat, I settled back to watch the England versus Paraguay World Cup match which was showing on the pub's television. After a fifteen minutes or so wait, a pretty, young waitress came to my table bearing a tray on which was my bar supper and a pint of beer. I pointed out that I had not ordered a pint, only to be told by the smiling girl that the pint and the meal were both on the house on account of my walk, compliments of the landlord. Unsought acts of kindness such as this one at the Ythan Arms, really made the very few bad days of walking which I had, seem worthwhile.

I had an early night that night. There was no problem in finding my bivouac as I was the only one on the campsite, which was probably just as well because in the morning I found the Gents toilet was locked and I had to surreptitiously make use of the Ladies. It was another hot, cloudless morning, and while I was packing my gear I debated for a while on following the long, sandy beach along the coast to Aberdeen. I had been told in the bar the previous night that this route was quite feasible, at least as far as Balmedie, as a number of locals had done a charity walk along the beach a couple of weeks earlier. However, I finally decided against it and headed off to tackle the day's relatively short mileage to Aberdeen where I had to call in at the lighthouse at Girdleness, after which I was planning on lying up for a couple of days rest at my brother's house in Bucksburn.

On leaving Newburgh I headed down the road and joined the A92 just past Foveran church. I took one look at the dense, speeding mass of traffic on this main route into the 'granite city', and very nearly did a complete about turn and re-traced my steps to Newburgh and the earlier discarded beach route. However, there was an alternative, and taking my life in my hands I managed to dash across the busy highway in a slight lull in the traffic, and I took to the back roads. These meandering, single-track country lanes, with their serpentine twists and turns would certainly add extra mileage onto my journey, but would at least improve my chances of arriving in Aberdeen on foot and not in the back of an ambulance.

It was quiet and tranquil walking along these hedgerow-lined little-used B roads, past ploughed fields of rich brown earth, and green, lush pastures being quietly grazed by cattle. This peace and complacency took a bit of a shattering just north of the village of Potterton though. I was passing a large luxurious looking house, probably an off-shoot of the oil

49

business I thought to myself, when all of a sudden a massive, jet-black alsatian dog, fangs gleaming and snarling murderously, came hurtling itself out of the house driveway at me. Luckily I was just out of range and the animal was abruptly brought up short by the thick chain attached to its spiked collar, but the incident left me feeling shaken and wondering if I had a clean change of underwear in my backpack.

I noticed throughout the walk that there is something about backpacking hikers that brings out the latent wolf in the most placid of domestic dogs. Perhaps the sight of the pack triggers some ancient, dormant memory of seeing off the itinerant pedlars and tinkers who used to roam the country in days gone by. Whatever it was, I never failed to be on the alert whenever I passed a roadside farm, for the inevitable piebald collie which would come yapping and snapping from its hideout in the byre. I've seen small, overfed poodles, safely behind walls in suburban gardens, going into a fit of rage and barking at my passing. Fortunately, I was never bitten, but I did have some very nasty moments. Besides the alsatian which I have just mentioned, I received a far worse fright on the road just south of Cockburnspath in Berwickshire. The road on which I was walking was situated on the crest of a slight elevation overlooking a field and a row of terraced houses. I happened to casually glance down and spotted two evil looking doberman pinschers clear in a single bound the mesh fence surrounding the garden of one of the houses, and begin to lope silently, and menacingly, across the field with yours truly the obvious target of their dubious affections.

I took the only possible evasive action I could at the time, and that was to quickly cross the extremely busy Berwick road and pray that my disappearing out of their line of vision, and the heavy traffic would deter them. The ploy worked but I found myself continuously looking over my shoulder for the next couple of miles.

Well, after my brush with the homicidal alsatian I stopped at a pub in Potterton to regain my composure before pushing on into the city.

Walking through the busy streets of Aberdeen I found that the mad hustle and bustle of the multitude going about their lawful business made me wish that I was back out on the quiet country roads, alsatians and all. Finally I crossed the bridge over the river Dee and walked through the old fisher district of Torry and on up to Girdleness lighthouse which stands on the low headland, towering above the golf course. Looking out to sea as I walked up the lighthouse road, I could see a mile or so off shore, four oil rigs lying idle, victims of the oil recession which was at that time really beginning to bite around the North East. For the past couple of days I had been witnessing a more human proof of the effect of this recession by the numerous houses bearing 'For Sale' placards which I continuously passed all along this part of the coast.

Girdleness lighthouse
courtesy Christopher
Nicholson

It was the tragic loss of the whaling ship *Oscar* with only two survivors out of a crew of forty-five, when the ship was smashed to pieces on the rocks of Girdleness, which caused the shipmasters of Aberdeen to demand that a lighthouse be erected to warn mariners of the headland. The lighthouse with its high tower, was duly established in 1833.

I found the two assistant lightkeepers painting the drainpipes on the station accommodation buildings, and I think my arrival provided a good enough excuse for them to down tools for the day. Assistant keeper Eric Bruce invited me into his house, telling me that the principal lightkeeper was away on holiday. I 'phoned up my brother to tell him of my arrival in the city, and then settled down to enjoy a chat and a can of beer with Eric, discovering that we had several friends in common. We had just finished the second tin when my brother arrived to drive me to his home in Bucksburn on the western outskirts of the city.

The remainder of that day, and all the next, I had designated as a rest period. This gave me the opportunity to launder my clothes and generally put things in order for the next stage of the walk.

While I was staying in Aberdeen, a certain anti-social aspect of long distance walking was brought to my attention. In the morning when I awoke at my brother's house, I searched high and low but I could not find my boots, until my sister-in-law Allison informed me that she had placed them outside on the window ledge.

... a certain anti-social aspect of long distance walking was brought to my attention ...

The next day I did some shopping and my laundry. In the afternoon I paid a visit to the Kirkgate bar which has long been a favourite meeting place of friends and acquaintances of mine who had left Thurso to live or work in Aberdeen, mainly in oil-related jobs. The locals call them the 'Caithness Mafia'. I was not disappointed in my visit and bumped into several old friends. Sadly, due to the oil recession, many of them had been recently laid off work. It would seem that the Aberdeen oil boom had finally burst, and not many of the people with whom I spoke were very optimistic of things picking up again in the immediate future.

Feeling well rested and with my backpack full of clean clothes once again, I bid farewell to my brother and his wife, and struck off down the A92, bound for the lighthouse at Tod Head, near Stonehaven. Although the road was busy there was a fine, broad verge to walk along and the traffic did not bother me at all. At Portlethen I was joined by a friend of mine, Marion Malcolm, who works as a nurse in Aberdeen, and had thought that the exercise would do her good.

We made pretty good time to Stonehaven, finding the town packed with people attending some kind of pageant. I never did discover what the event was all about, but there were a great many vintage cars about the town, and the local police were dressed up in Victorian uniforms.

On the outskirts of Stonehaven we passed the imposing, sea-cliff stronghold of Dunottar castle. During the Reformation in 1651, it was here that the governor of the castle, George Ogilvie, kept the regalia of the Scottish crown jewels safe from the clutches of Oliver Cromwell.

A couple of miles past Dunottar we quit the main road to walk along the quiet country lanes past fields of oil-seed rape which gleamed with such an intense yellow glow that it almost hurt your eyes to gaze upon them. Shortly we arrived at the village of Catterline, a place once very popular with artists. The village pub, the Creel Inn, was open and a more than welcome sight after another hot and dusty day. This was the night of the England versus Argentina World Cup football game, and I noticed that there was a large colour television set up in the bar for the patrons to enjoy the game. In fact it seemed that the majority of people in the pub, including the landlord, were Englishmen. This had its advantages, because when England scored what was to be their only goal of the match, the landlord let out a whoop of delight and promptly poured out a large measure of malt whisky for everyone in the bar. I took a sip of the free drink and muttered to Marion that I sincerely hoped that the game would be decided on penalties. Unfortunately for England it wasn't, and Argentina, helped by Maradona's 'hand of God', won two one.

Marion left to hitch a lift back to Aberdeen, and I took to the narrow country lanes to walk the remainder of the way to Tod Head. I had been told that there was a shorter cliff-top route to the lighthouse from Catterline, but in the gathering dark, and with the malt whisky glowing inside me, I thought it more prudent to stick to the roads. The word 'Tod' is the old Scottish name for the fox, and this area certainly looked like fox country. If indeed it was, then old Reynard could have had himself an easy meal that night. As I approached the lighthouse, I passed a field full of partridges. The birds were so engrossed in their business that I was able to get within a few feet of them before they took alarm and flew off.

Although it is situated on a cliff-top on the rugged coast, the stubby lighthouse of Tod Head presents quite a pastoral rather than a nautical scene, being surrounded to landward by rich, arable farmlands. This lighthouse was built in 1897, and is a one-man operated station, or rather was, as I hear that it has been automated since my visit. On my arrival I

Todhead lighthouse
courtesy Northern Lighthouse Board

was warmly greeted by principal lightkeeper Magnus Pearson who introduced me to his young sons and his wife Fiona who kindly made me some supper before I retired to the bothy for a good night's sleep.

In the morning, Magnus gave me a guided tour of Tod Head lighthouse station, and then accompanied me for the first couple of miles along the quiet back roads. He pointed out to me the old church at Kinneff where the Scottish crown jewels lay buried until the Restoration. They had been eventually smuggled out of the besieged Dunottar castle by the wife of Kinneff's minister who had concealed them in a bundle of flax. Magnus turned back for the lighthouse at Kinneff, and I pushed on to join up with the main road. The traffic was surprisingly light, and I headed south under clear blue skies, the good weather was still holding.

By mid-morning I was walking through Inverbervie, an old town which was granted a royal charter as far back as 1341 when David II, king of Scotland, was forced to take shelter with his ship in the harbour after coming off the worse in a scrap with a much larger English fleet. I was due to meet the ladies of the local lifeboat guild here, but due to a mix-up about the time of my arrival in the town, I was sad to say I completely missed them. This was not the case on the stretch of road between Inverbervie and St. Cyrus however, as I was ambushed no less than twice by ladies of the local lifeboat guilds. The first group I encountered were the ladies of the village of Gourdon who cheered me on my way waving RNLI flags and presenting me with a poster which stated: 'BEST OF LUCK ON YOUR WALK. GOURDON LADIES LIFEBOAT GUILD.' A few miles further on from this encounter, I was met by the ladies lifeboat guild from the village of Johnshaven. Stopping for five minutes I had an interesting chat with Mrs. Ross who was the president of the area guild. Mrs. Ross was a retired chiropodist, and I told her that I wished I had met her a couple of weeks ago when my blisters were to the fore. These had fortunately healed by now, and I am glad to say that I was never to be bothered by this particular vexation again.

It had been yet another roasting hot morning's walk, and on arriving in St. Cyrus in the early afternoon, I stopped at the St. Cyrus Hotel for a quick intake of liquids and a couple of packets of salted peanuts, which I had recently taken to eating. I had a very good reason behind this sudden fad for salted peanuts, which I will explain. Almost every day since the day I arrived in Lossiemouth, the weather had either been blazing hot and sunny, or clammy and humid. I had discovered one night when pitching my bivouac that I kept suffering agonizing cramps in my hands. I mentioned this to my brother when I was in Aberdeen, and we both came to the same conclusion. I was suffering from a salt deficiency having sweated so much each day walking with a heavy pack in the heat. So this became my remedy, eat a couple of packets of salted peanuts each day. It must have done the trick because I was never troubled with the cramps again.

St. Cyrus is renowned for its nature reserve which is reputed to have over 300 different varieties of native wild flowers. To pass the time on my walk from the town to nearby Montrose, I tried to list mentally as many British wild flowers as I could. I remembered quite a few, but nowhere near 300.

I arrived in Montrose late that afternoon. The man who I personally regard as the greatest military leader ever produced by Scotland, was born in and took his title from this town. James Graham, Marquis of Montrose. The military career of this remarkable man started when he took up the Covenant cause. Covenant troops led by him took and occupied Aberdeen no less than three times, inflicting a memorable and crushing defeat on Viscount Aboyne and the government forces at the Battle of Bridge of Dee in 1639. But Montrose could never get on or agree with the dour and scheming Archibald Duke of Argyle, nor would he join in full insurrection against his king. When the Civil War broke out he left the Covenanters to embrace the Royalist cause and virtually conquered the whole of Scotland for Charles I. However, with the debacle of the Battle of Worcester, and other defeats and disasters for the Royalist cause south of the border, all was lost and Montrose was forced to go into exile.

His final battle occurred when he was ill-advisedly persuaded back to Scotland in the cause of the exiled Charles II. Leading a poorly equipped and half-trained army, he was soundly defeated at the Battle of Carbisdale. A fugitive, Montrose sought shelter with Macleod of Assynt, who treacherously handed him over to the searching government forces. He was then taken to Edinburgh and executed at the Tolbooth by order of his old adversary the Duke of Argyle.

I suppose that the ghost of Montrose must have had the last laugh though. A short time later with the restoration of Charles II, the Duke of Argyle was himself to meet the same fate at the Edinburgh Tolbooth.

I was walking along the main street of Montrose, pondering on the vagaries and misfortunes of history, when I was suddenly hijacked by two gentlemen of the press. They bundled me into their car to take me to the local lifeboat shed for photographs, and then had me pose for the snap which was eventually printed in the papers, standing with Scurdie Ness lighthouse in the background. One of this dynamic duo asked me a number of questions about the walk so far, and then they both promptly disappeared, presumably into the nearest pub where I think they must

The author with Scurdie Ness lighthouse in the background
courtesy The Courier, *Dundee*

have been lying in wait all afternoon for my arrival. I actually read the article which they did on me in the Dundee Courier, and in which they aged me five years and reported that I had told them that I had walked through a blizzard on my way to Inverness.

Before checking in at Scurdie Ness lighthouse, I stopped in the neighbouring village of Ferryden for a meal in the South Esk Hotel. This establishment used to be the famous 'Diamond Lil's'. Lil was renowned for her eccentricity of refusing to have anything to do with decimal currency. If you wanted a drink you had to pay for it in pounds, shillings and pence. Changed days here now though. A very attractive young barmaid called Cathy was serving behind the bar, and she gave me a free pint of beer when she heard about my walk, as well as taking a sponsor form for the pub's locals to contribute.

It was about a mile walk from the South Esk Hotel to Scurdie Ness lighthouse. The lighthouse built in 1870 looks down on the shifting sand banks of the narrow estuary mouth, out of which in 1716 James, the Old Pretender, and the bumbling Earl of Mar, sailed off into ignominious exile after the defeats of Sherrifmuir and Preston.

Scurdie Ness lighthouse
courtesy John Wilkie

The principal lightkeeper at Scurdie Ness was Bob Duthie who greeted me on arrival and invited me up to his house where Mrs. Duthie had my second meal of that evening waiting for me. Without even flinching, I scoffed the lot. Hungry work this walking. I had last seen Bob in 1979 when he had been the principal lightkeeper at Inchkeith lighthouse in the Firth of Forth, and I had been spending a few weeks there as a relieving keeper. We sat and yarned for a good while, until I had to excuse myself and went and got my head down for the night in the lighthouse bothy.

A sound night's sleep in the bothy, followed by a breakfast of mammoth proportions, courtesy of Mrs. Duthie, put me in fighting fettle for the next leg of the trip. For the next few nights I would be relying on the bivouac as I did not have another lighthouse to call upon until the one at Barns Ness, near Dunbar. I would, however, be stopping off for a day or two in Edinburgh where I was due to call in at the Northern Lighthouse Board headquarters and see the Board's General Manager Commander John Mackay.

Bob Duthie kept me company along the road to Ferryden but declined my invitation to push on to Edinburgh with me. To avoid the heavy traffic on the main roads, I took to the country lanes. I had several options and I was not really sure of my eventual destination that day, so I decided to just push on and see where I ended up.

The road meandered through woodlands, and a thick, murky haar, blown inland off the North Sea, gave an eerie aspect to the twisted and gnarled branches of the trees. At times the visibility was little more than twenty yards and I was thankful that the traffic was almost non-existent. The air was full of tiny drops of moisture which coalesced and streamed off my waterproofs. A slight puff of wind completely cleared the haar as I passed the sandy shores of Lunan Bay. I could clearly see the ruins of Red castle, once owned by Robert the Bruce. The reason for the castle's name was quite apparent in the crumbling ruins which were the colour of paprika. No sooner had I passed the castle when the haar came swirling back again, blocking all from view but the immediate road in front of me.

The day continued with rapidly changing states of visibility as a contrary breeze blew the grey mist this way and that. At the village of Marywell I rejoined the main road, walking well up on the roadside verge, as large lorries came thundering out of the murk. Although it was wisely in the interests of self-preservation to walk on the verge, it did have its setbacks. It must have been quite some time since the local council's hedging and ditching gang had been around this way, as the grass and weeds came well up to mid-thigh. This not only severely hampered progress, but left my feet and legs absolutely soaking.

My arrival at the town of Arbroath brought easier and drier progress as I moved off the grass and onto the pavement. By this time the sun was burning off the haar, and was shining dully through the greyness.

Arbroath was originally called Aberbrothock, which sounds like an ancient Celtic obscenity if you say it fast.

As all good Scots should know, the abbey here built by William the Lion as a tribute to Thomas Becket, was where the famous Declaration of Arbroath was sent to Pope John XXII in April 1320 in an attempt to counter Edward of England's diplomatic machinations to have Robert the Bruce excommunicated.

I stopped here briefly for something to eat and drinkr. On my way out of the town I looked to seaward to see if I could catch a glimpse of the Bell Rock lighthouse, but although the haar had now completely cleared from the land, it still hung over the sea like a thick, grey curtain. I did notice the old Bell Rock lighthouse signal station as I walked past. This is now used as a museum, and I would have liked to have dropped in and taken a look around as I did two separate tours of duty on the Bell Rock when I was a supernumary lightkeeper, but the volume of traffic put me off trying to cross the road to visit the place.

The bulk of the afternoon was spent dodging traffic on the busy A92, until thoroughly fed up and almost a nervous wreck, I took the turn off for Carnoustie, thinking to stay there overnight.

This was golf links country, and army training territory with the nearby range of Barry Buddon. I remember going shooting on the ranges here during my navy days. We would all gleefully pile into the back of a navy lorry and be driven here from Rosyth dockyard. The army would always be conspicuous by their absence whenever we had a day at the range. Not that I blame them, a gang of matelots armed with rifles and live ammunition must have been a prospect quite wearing on the nerves of even the toughest RSM.

I could not find the campsite which was marked on my map at Carnoustie, and on asking in one of the local pubs, I was told that the place was now a building site. I experienced a flutter of notoriety in the pub when the barman said that he recognized me from my picture in the local paper. This was good for a free pint and directions to the nearest campsite in nearby Monifieth.

The evening was wearing on so I pushed on for Monifieth without delay, arriving there quite late in the evening and dog-tired. I entered the campsite and finding a quiet spot I erected the bivouac and was quickly off to sleep. It rained quite heavily that night, and although on wakening up the next morning I discovered a small pool of water just inside the entrance of the bivouac, all else seemed quite watertight.

This was the morning when I was fated to meet the one really obnoxious person of the entire trip. Apparently I had pitched my bivouac on a residential caravan site in mistake for the official council campsite, which was only a short distance away but I had missed it in the dark. Just as I had finished packing my gear, a large, red-faced, fat lady appeared on the scene and pointed out the error of my ways with such vehemence that I found it impossible to get a word in edgeways.

"This is a private site!" she shouted. "It will cost you four pounds for camping illegally here!" she screeched. "I do not allow dogs or campers on my caravan site!" she howled.

... 'I do not allow dogs or campers on my caravan site!' ...

So full of her own self-righteous indignation was this bespectacled lump of obesity, that it was impossible to explain or reason with her. I paid her the four pounds, well worth it to shut her up if nothing else, and I was by this time so incensed myself by this harpy, that I left without taking change from the five pound note which I handed her. I remember noticing at the time that the woman was wearing a Celtic cross on a chain around her flabby neck, and thinking to myself that this person was neither a Celt or a Christian.

As the saying goes, it only takes one person to give a place a bad name. From that morning onwards I found myself regarding that pleasant little Angus town not as Monifieth, but 'Money thief'.

Not in the best of humours I headed out of Monifieth determined to arrive at the Tay road bridge as soon as possible and put another barrier beetween me and the place. I stopped briefly at Broughty Ferry to visit the bank and boost my sadly depleted funds.

I did not enjoy that morning's walk, taking me as it did through mainly built up areas on the outskirts of Dundee, and then through the city itself until I reached the bridge. To my mind Dundee is a grim town with an even grimmer history of massacre and bloodshed which goes back as far as 834 when the defeated Alpin king of the Scots was beheaded by the victorious Brude king of the Picts, on Dundee Law.

Edward of England sacked the town in 1291, and it was during the subsequent English occupation that a promising young lad called William Wallace was reputed to have stabbed to death the son of Selby the English constable. Wallace was forced to flee for his life, but he returned a few years later at the head of a Scottish army which took the town again for Scotland. In 1385 Richard II of England burned Dundee to the ground, and Henry VIII was only just diverted from emulating Richard, when after his victory at the Battle of Pinkie he received news that Mary of Guise was planning on sending a joint Franco-Scottish force against him.

Dundee became a hot-bed of the Covenanters, so much so that it was nicknamed the 'Scottish Geneva'. In 1645 the Marquis of Montrose took the town by storm with an army of 750 men, mainly Highlanders, but before the real fun of plunder, arson and rape could get under way, Montrose received news that a large Covenanting army under the joint command of Baillie and Harvie was on its way to relieve the town, and Montrose was forced, with great difficulty, to gather his men together and retreat.

A few years later during the Civil War, Dundee became a Royalist stronghold. Cromwell sent General Monk north to subdue the town, which he duly did with the brutality characteristic of the times. The heavily outnumbered Royalist troops under the command of Major General Lumsden, who were garrisoning the town, surrendered. Monk had them butchered to a man, and then turned loose his own blood-crazed troops in an orgy of violence on the Dundee streets. After the event it was found that fully one sixth of the unarmed civilian population had been murdered.

John Graham of Claverhouse, 'Bonnie Dundee', unsuccessfully attempted an assault on the town from which he took the title of his viscountcy, in 1689. The assault was repulsed but not until after Claverhouse had succeeded in burning down the suburb of Hilltown. Dundee last fell to military might in 1745 when Sir John Kinloch and a small Jacobite force took and held the town for Prince Charles for a short time.

To add to this grim catalogue of warfare, there are also natural catastrophes to consider such as the Tay Bridge disaster on the night of 28th

December 1879. The rail bridge over the river Tay collapsed and 75 people perished when the train which was crossing the bridge at the time plunged into the storm tossed waters of the Firth. The sole survivor of the tragedy was a small spaniel dog which somehow managed to swim ashore on that terrible night. Among other disasters, there was always of course, Maconnagal.

It was with a sense of relief that I climbed up onto the Tay road bridge which has a pedestrian walkway running along the centre between the northbound and southbound lanes of traffic. Up here, out over the water there was a gentle, cool breeze blowing in off the North Sea which helped to clear my head of the stink of the city and exhaust fumes.

I left the bridge and entered the Kingdom of Fife, where according to the song, the diminutive barrel maker with a predilection for bestiality and sadism, came from. (Work that one out for yourself.)

To celebrate crossing the Tay I stopped off at a pub in Newport-on-Tay for a bar lunch and pint of beer. Over my meal I consulted my map. My options were open for that afternoon, I could either head across country for the town of Cupar and hope to find somewhere to camp for the night there, or I could keep to the coast and make for St. Andrews, both routes being the same mileage. I opted in the end for the coastal route, and left the pub heading for the headquarters of golf.

The weather had turned hot again and the sun beat down upon me as I walked past bramble-dotted hedgerows. It was certainly warm enough here but I dreaded to think how hot I would have been without the benefit of the slight cool breeze off the sea.

I soldiered onwards, steadily eating up the miles. I would stop every three quarters of an hour for a five minute rest in the shade of the hedgerow, and a quick smoke. Aircraft from RAF Leuchars occasionally streaked overhead, evoking memories of the Moray Firth coast. Pop music hummed softly from my backpack, interrupted every few seconds by the high-pitched 'bleep' caused by the radar situated at the end of the runway at RAF Leuchars. I crossed the river Eden at Guardbridge, the still waters looking cool and inviting on that scorching hot summer's day.

It was a weary walk from Guardbridge to St. Andrews on a narrow-verged road and facing a heavy stream of almost continuous traffic coming from Scotland's oldest university city and 'Mecca' of the golfing fraternity. I was very nearly run over by nothing less than a Rolls Royce on this stretch of road, which I suppose has a bit more class about it than being spattered all over the tarmac by a proletarian Metro.

St. Andrews is steeped in history. They do say that it is the most haunted town in Scotland. The story which I like best is the highly dubious tale about the founding of the town. It is said that St. Rule of Patras, which is where St. Andrew was martyred, was shipwrecked here in the assorted company of a priest, two deacons, eight hermits, and three devout virgins. This colourful crew were escorting a bizarre collection of holy relics of the dead St. Andrew, which consisted of the saint's arm-bone, three fingers off the right hand, a tooth, and a knee cap. A local Pictish king called Angus witnessed the shipwreck and quickly arrived on the scene to plunder the wreckage. However, Angus had a vision of a white cross in the blue sky, which caused him to mend his ways and adopt St. Andrew as his patron saint.

The university was authorized by papal decree in 1413.

I cannot logically explain why, but I took an instant dislike to the place as soon as I entered the town. Maybe one of St. Andrew's many ghosts was walking at my side, but I felt distinctly uneasy and regretting that I had not stuck to my original plan and walked to Cupar.

Over a cool pint of beer in a pub full of university types, I consulted my map and conceived the idea of catching a bus to Anstruther. The bus ride would not be cheating on my walk as Anstruther and St. Andrews were both equidistant from Kirkcaldy which was my planned destination for the following day. There was also a lifeboat station at Anstruther, and I had promised to call at as many stations as I could.

I did not have long to wait for a bus, Anstruther being on a local service route. In fact I quite enjoyed the meandering journey around the East Neuk of Fife, and I was almost sorry when we arrived at our destination. This was the night of the World Cup semi-final between France and West Germany. I was eager to watch this match, and on my arrival I immediately sought out a pub with a television in it. I found what I wanted in an establishment called the Ship Inn, and I settled down in a seat with a good view, a pint of beer and a bag of crisps close at hand. The 'Auld Alliance' has certainly not been forgotten in Fife, as I found that everybody in the pub was vociferously supporting the French. Unfortunately it was to no avail as they lost, and on the full time whistle I left the Ship Inn, leaving the locals to mutter into their pints and nips about the terrible standard of World Cup football refereeing.

Anstruther has a couple of connections with the lighthouse service. In the scenic little harbour here is berthed the old North Carr lightship, the last lightship to be in service with the Northern Lighthouse Board, and now serving as a floating exhibit. The other connection is a little more bizarre. It was in Anstruther where Eppie Laing was burned at the stake for reputedly causing a terrible storm by witchcraft in which was drowned the architect of an early lighthouse on the Isle of May.

Due to a bit of misunderstanding, I failed to get in touch with the local lifeboat people. It was getting late by now and I had yet to find somewhere to camp for the night. After my experience in Monifieth you can bet that I was going to be absolutely certain about where I put up my bivouac. I was told that there was an official campsite at nearby St. Monans, and so that is where I headed, arriving at about eleven o'clock that evening and falling into a deep, exhausted sleep as soon as I had erected the bivouac.

St. Monans was called after the saint of the same name, there once being a shrine in memory of the saint situated here. David II, king of Scotland popularized the place for a time when he ordered a church to be built at the shrine in thanks to the saint for his complete recovery from a rather nasty arrow wound.

A swelteringly hot morning found me sitting on a wall outside of a St. Monans general store, drinking a pint of cool milk for breakfast while I idly watched an elderly lollipop man fussily directing schoolchildren across an almost traffic-free road. During a quiet spell he sauntered over to me and declared that he recognized my face from a picture in the Dundee Courier. Ah, all this fame!

There was more to follow, as a few minutes later the local postman came up to me, and with outstretched hand said: "Fancy meeting you here. I'm the part time attendant of the automatic lighthouse at Elie. I saw your photo in the Courier." I sat and chatted to these two worthies for a short while before bidding them farewell and pushing on for Kirkcaldy.

The heat of the day cast a blue-grey haze over the waters of the Firth of Forth, completely obscuring the Lothian shore. I paused frequently to take a refreshing drink from an outsize bottle of lemonade which I had bought in St. Monans and somehow or other managed to jam into my already full backpack. On the outskirts of Earlsferry I was overtaken by two lady joggers, looking very natty in their designer tracksuits. I do not think that this pair were overly dedicated athletes, as I nearly overtook them on the first hill we encountered.

At midday I stopped at Upper Largo. The Largo area of Fife held a special interest for me because it was from this area that my grandmother came. She died when I was quite young and I do not remember her, but I found it interesting to see the place where one of my immediate ancestors grew up. I glanced up at the gorse-dotted eminence of Largo Law and wondered wistfully if granny had often climbed up there as a young girl to gaze out on the ships in the Forth.

Largo is known for its connections with two famous Scottish seamen. Alexander Selkirk, who was born here in 1676, is probably the more widely known of the two. Selkirk was the sailing master on board a ship called the *Cinque Ports* when he had a difference of opinion with the ship's captain, a man called Stradling. It must have been a pretty heated quarrel because Stradling ended up by marooning Selkirk on the uninhabited Pacific island of Juan Fernandez, where the Fifer was to live in solitude for four years and four months before his eventual rescue by a passing ship. When he heard the story, the author Daniel Defoe based his character of Robinson Crusoe on Alexander Selkirk.

The other famous seaman lies buried in Largo. This is Sir Andrew Wood who was probably Scotland's greatest admiral. His most famous victory was in 1489 when in his flagship *Yellow Caravell* he led the Scottish forces in a resounding defeat of a far larger English fleet which had sailed up the Firth of Forth. He finished his days in Largo where he had a canal dug from his house to the local church and had his servants row him along it in a boat, to attend services.

Leaving Largo behind me I followed the road as it curved around the sandy sweep of Largo Bay and entered the eastern end of the central Scotland industrial belt with the adjoining towns and built up areas of Leven, Buckhaven and Methil. Leven was once one of the most important coal exporting ports in Scotland until shifting sands completely blocked the harbour. I hurried on through this area as quickly as possible, stopping only briefly at a Ladbrokes betting shop in Methil where on a whim I bet three pounds worth of my free bet vouchers on a horse called 'Try to stop me'.

The afternoon walk took me past Wemyss castle where Darnley originally popped the question to Mary Queen of Scots back in February 1565. The disc jockey on Radio Forth kept gibbering something about the hottest day of the year, as I slunk into the 'lang toon' of Kirkcaldy.

Due to the past few days of sleeping rough in the bivouac at night, and sweating in the sweltering heat as I walked during the day, I was now quite badly in need of a bath. With this end in mind, I opted to go bed and breakfast that night and found digs in Kirkcaldy at 49 Mitchel Street where after the luxury of a hot shower, it was a quiet night watching the telly and then early to bed between clean, white sheets instead of my distinctly aromatic sleeping bag.

To my eternal shame I have completely forgotten the name of the charming landlady at 49 Mitchel Street. I mention this because when I came to settle up for my night's board, she steadfastly refused my money, telling me to accept the free bed and breakfast as her donation towards my sponsored walk.

On buying a daily paper after I left my night's lodgings, I was delighted to see in the racing results that my funds had been further boosted by the horse 'Try to stop me', winning the race at the handsome odds of five to one. Adam Smith the famous eighteenth century economist was born in Kirkcaldy in 1723. I wonder if this had any influence on my sudden riches?

Leaving Kirkcaldy I walked past the huge industrial complex of the Seafield colliery. I had always thought that the town's prosperity was based on coal, but funnily enough I found out later that this was not exactly the cause, but that Kirkcaldy was world famous for the manufacture of linoleum.

It was yet another scorcher of a day as I followed the coast road, the Forth still obscured by haze. On the outskirts of Kinghorn I passed the roadside memorial which commemorates a tragic incident long ago which was to have far reaching consequences for Scotland. The memorial marks the spot where in 1265 king Alexander III's horse lost its footing and threw the king over the cliff, the subsequent fall breaking his neck. It was a stormy night and Alexander had been travelling against the advice of his leading men, eager to spend the night in Dunfermline with Queen Yolette, his bride of just four months. His death ended two hundred years of relative peace and prosperity for Scotland, as it encouraged Edward of England to meddle in the succession crisis which Alexander's death brought about, and to subsequently try and take over the entire country.

A couple of miles further along the coast, I stopped briefly at Burntisland where, according to legend, Agricola had a naval base in AD 83. Cromwell paid a visit to the neighbourhood in 1651 during which he destroyed with a single cannon shot, the provost of Burntisland's china shop, which speedily convinced the provost of the error of his ways in supporting the Royalist cause.

As I trudged along the shore of the Forth that day, I was debating with myself as to where I would spend the approaching evening. My first two choices had been to stop at either Dunfermline or Inverkeithing, but then I hit upon the idea of 'phoning my head office and asking them to contact the Royal Navy and ask them if it would be possible for me to spend the night at the navy signal station at North Queensferry. I had worked as a signalman in the navy myself, and I thought that the navy might regard this idea as good public relations. I stopped off at the village of Aberdour — where Sir Patrick Spens went walking on the strand — and from the pub I 'phoned up headquarters who thought it a reasonable idea and asked me to ring back in an hour. This hour quickly passed in the convivial atmosphere of the Aberdour pub, and I contacted George Street again to see how they had got on with my request. I was told that when the navy was contacted about my request, they did not exactly give an outright refusal, but nobody was prepared to take the responsibility of making a decision about the matter. This news did not really surprise me over much, as I said earlier, I was in the navy once myself.

Leaving Aberdour I resolved to make for Inverkeithing where I decided that due to my happy financial state at the present time, I would endeavour again to find a bed and breakfast billet for the night. Approaching Hillend I became entangled in the streams of traffic and people knocking off work and heading home from the industrial estate. It was Friday night and they stopped for no man. I noticed a bed and breakfast sign outside the Hillend Tavern, about a mile from Inverkeithing, and on making enquiries in the pub, I found that they had a vacancy, so I decided to stop there.

I unpacked my gear in the neat and tidy little bedroom above the pub bar which I had been allocated, and then I luxuriated in a piping hot bath, washing away the dirt, dust and grime of yet another hot day's walk. Feeling refreshed after my long soak, I left the digs and strolled into the neighbouring town of Inverkeithing to search out something to eat, and to take a nostalgic trip down memory lane. During my naval career I had often been stationed at nearby Rosyth. In fact the last ship I had served on in the royal navy, the minelayer *HMS Abdiel*, was still operating out of this port. On shore leave at Rosyth, my mates and I would spend much of our time in Inverkeithing, or 'Inverqueerthing' as we irreverently called the place.

They do say that you should never return to places that you once knew well because they never appear the same as you remember them. That night I discovered the truth of this adage. The last time I had been in Inverkeithing was in November 1976, when I had been involved in a riotous session in the bar of the Central Hotel, celebrating my two hour old civilian status.

After a meal at a nearby cafe which appeared to have changed little in the intervening ten years, I headed across the road to re-acquaint myself with the Central. The exterior of the pub looked just the same, but inside things were totally different. Extensive alterations and modernization had altered, and to my mind completely killed off, the whole character of the place. After just one pint of gassy, lukewarm beer, I returned to the Hillend Tavern feeling just a little bit sad and disillusioned.

I should mention here that Inverkeithing has another famous connection with the navy, not the royal navy though, but the Russian navy. Sir Samuel Grieg who was the founder of the Russian navy back in the eighteenth century, was born in the town in 1735. It is interesting to note that the modern, mighty, nuclear fleets of both the super powers, the USA and USSR had in the persons of John Paul Jones and Samuel Grieg, both been originally founded by Scotsmen.

Back at the Hillend Tavern it seemed to be party time. The bar was crowded and disco music from the sixties blared out above the noisy chatter and clinking of glasses. I discovered that the local village gala was to be held on the following day, and many of the local residents were determined to start the celebrations now. I scooted off to my bed at eleven o'clock, which was probably quite a sensible thing to do as the party just seemed to be getting in to full swing about then.

On rising the next morning I had a quick wash and packed my gear. These tasks completed I left my room and was greeted by the landlord's wife who was getting herself into a bit of a panic over breakfast as she had mislaid her husband who seemingly had the only set of keys to the pantry in his pocket. He was eventually discovered to be locked in the pub downstairs where he was having his own private party in celebration of the gala.

Over breakfast — sausage, bacon, eggs, and toast for myself; tin of beer for the landlord — I swapped a Northern Lighthouse Board uniform cap

. . . then the ultimate in fame happened . . .

badge with him in exchange for his promise to put one of my sponsor forms around his pub's locals. Then the ultimate in fame happened, the landlord's young daughter asked me for my autograph!

The brightly coloured gala day flags and bunting hung limply in the still air of yet another scorching day as I shouldered my backpack and strode out of Hillend to negotiate the minor spaghetti junction of roads which lead onto the approaches to the Forth road bridge. It was thankfully a Saturday morning, and in consequence the early traffic was a lot lighter than it would have been on a working day when hundreds of cars would have been commuting across the Forth to Edinburgh. As it was, it was busy enough.

I began to cross the bridge's one and three quarter mile span of the Firth of Forth. One of my first views as I looked below me from the height of the bridge, was the white painted signal station at North Queensferry where I had hoped to spend the previous night. Further along the bridge I glanced over the safety rail and noticed out on the still waters of the Forth, the sleek, grey shape of a naval frigate heading leisurely out to the North Sea. The weather, even well out over the cool water, was sweltering; and there was a smoky-blue haze obscuring Edinburgh from view.

Upon successfully reaching the Lothian shore of the Forth, I was confronted by the colourful sight of dozens of cyclists, many in fancy dress, with balloons and streamers trailing from the handlebars of their bikes. I recalled hearing on Radio Forth earlier that morning that there was a planned bike ride to St. Andrews from Edinburgh to be held that day, and I was now encountering the front runners. In fact I was to pass stragglers all the way to the outskirts of the city proper. I thought, perhaps a bit uncharitably at the time, that some of the worthies I passed looked highly unlikely to even reach the Forth Road Bridge, let alone St. Andrews.

There is really little to write about the remainder of that day's walk as it was mainly just a weary procession through the city streets until I arrived at my digs in the city centre. It was a far from pleasant journey, and the combination of burning hot sun, city grime, stinking exhaust fumes, and bustling humanity, did little to ease the way.

Gratefully I finally reached the city centre and Lothian Road where I presented myself to Rachel Argo, one of the Northern Lighthouse Board's headquarters staff, who was to be my landlady until the Monday morning when I was to meet the Board's General Manager, and representatives of the RNLI Scotland. Rachel greeted me and immediately offered me a cool tin of beer out of the fridge. An extremely intuitive and discerning lady I thought.

I hadn't had far to walk that day and it was still only mid-afternoon, so after a hot bath and a change of clothes, I decided to go out for a wander about the capital. The hot weather had brought the female population of Edinburgh out in their scantiest summer dresses, shorts, and in some cases even swimsuits. I spent the best part of an hour indulging in a spate of good, old-fashioned lechery as I sauntered up and down Prince's Street and idled about the neighbouring gardens. Eventually feeling bored with this pastime, I headed for an Indian restaurant which I knew, to enjoy a first-class curry.

That evening I had arranged to meet an old friend of mine, Sandra Budge. Sandra is the daughter of a fellow lightkeeper Tom Budge who was up in Shetland with me for a few years. Tom was transferred to the Isle of Skye, but Sandra stayed on in Shetland with my wife and myself until she had finished her final year at school in Lerwick.

Sandra has a bright and bubbly sense of humour which has never failed to cheer me up; she is also very pretty. This was just the kind of company I was needing after the dreadful morning's walk, and I met her that evening in the Green Tree pub in Edinburgh's Cowgate. From this starting point we enjoyed a pub crawl around the Cowgate and the adjacent Grassmarket — pubs which are just renowned for the quality of the cask conditioned ales they sell.

I have always enjoyed wandering around this old area of the city of Edinburgh. There is a distinct atmosphere about the place, and in the air you can almost sense a tangible reek of the turbulent and often gory history of the area. With the dark bulk of the castle glowering down from the high rock, you can almost picture the villainous 'Resurrectionists' Burke and Hare going about their grisly business among the shadowy vennels and wynds; or perhaps catch a glimpse of the unfortunate

Porteous at the head of the town guard; or the seemingly respectable Deacon Brodie heading home to change into his nocturnal burglar's attire.

With no walking to do the next day, I did not say goodnight to Sandra and head back to my lodgings until two o'clock in the morning, where I enjoyed a good night's sleep with the benefit of a long lie-in on the Sunday morning. Rachel Argo kindly gave me the use of her automatic washing machine and tumble drier, and so I passed a good part of that day catching up with my laundry. That evening I went out for a meal and watched the World Cup final in one of the Grassmarket pubs which had an outsize television screen fitted up for the occasion. After the match I headed off to bed so as to be well refreshed and ready for the next leg of my journey on the morrow.

Before beginning the day's walk I first called in at headquarters at 84 George Street where I met the Board's General Manager Commander John Mackay. We chatted about the progress of the walk so far, and I was introduced to two very senior gentlemen from the Scottish RNLI headquarters who generously presented me with a couple of Lifeboat T-shirts. Not to be upstaged, the secretary of the Lighthouse Board conjured up an anniversary lighthouse tie for me.

Commander Mackay signed my check-in sheet, and photographs were duly taken by a gentleman from the Edinburgh Evening News. It had been hoped that the BBC television Scotland would have been present, but I was upstaged by a meeting in Edinburgh that day of the Scottish Labour Party MPs who were busy putting the country to rights. I seemed to be jinxed with television coverage of my walk. I was told when I was travelling around the north-east that Grampian television were eager to interview me. This had to be postponed when the camera crews were diverted to Fraserburgh to film Prince Philip who was, ironically enough, launching a new lifeboat.

I stopped for a while and chatted to several of the headquarters staff, and would have liked to linger a lot longer, but I still had a full day's walking ahead of me and time was getting on. My pack on my back, I threaded my way through the bustling city streets, heading east.

The South . . .

Changes of coasts and border interlude

 HEADING out of Edinburgh I walked through the exotically named districts of Portobello and Joppa. I do not know how Joppa obtained its name, but Portobello was so christened by a sailor called George Hamilton who when he retired built a house here on what was then the outskirts of the city. He named the house after Puerto Bello in Panama where he had fought with the naval forces under the command of Admiral Vernon.

At Musselburgh, which is reputed to have been a seaport since Roman times, I was faced with one of the stiffest tests of my self-discipline so far. As I have mentioned previously, one of the great loves of my life is horse racing, and I discovered that today was the date of the monthly Edinburgh race meeting at Musselburgh racecourse. My idea of paradise would be something of a cross between Goodwood and Newmarket, with a bit of Cheltenham thrown in for the winter, and it took a great effort of will to walk past this flat, green racecourse on the shores of the Firth of Forth, but walk past it I did.

Along the coast from Musselburgh is Prestonpans where one morning in 1745 General Sir John Cope was rudely awoken from his sleep to find his redcoats being routed by the Jacobite army; and to the landward side of the road which I was walking, lay the site of the battle of Pinkie where the English army under the command of Henry VIII had defeated the Scottish forces.

Indeed many battles and skirmishes had been fought in this area, and countless armies and smaller bodies of armed men had preceded me along this particular road which had once been the principal invasion and counter invasion route with the 'auld enemy' England.

I had been looking forward to a brief stop in Tranent for a dinner time pint, but due to road works I found myself on the new by-pass which missed the town by about half a mile. I had to content myself with a ten minute rest and a smoke, sitting atop a lay-by litter bin.

It was another hot day, and although I appreciate a spell of fine weather as much as the next person, I was beginning to find the continuous sunshine a bit tiring and monotonous, and I do not think I would have been too upset to have been subjected to a good going blizzard for a day or two.

By early evening I had arrived at the town of Haddington, feeling hot, hungry and thirsty. I had planned to camp somewhere in the Haddington area for the night, and over a meal and a pint in the George Hotel, I chatted to several of the very friendly locals, trying to find a place where I might set up my bivouac for the night. I was told that there was an excellent campsite at Monksmuir, a couple of miles to the east of Haddington. As I was feeling much refreshed and rested after my meal and a pint, I decided to push on to this campsite, enjoying the walk in the cool of the evening.

The Monksmuir campsite was beautifully situated amidst groves of broad-leafed trees. The place was immaculately clean with a well-looked after, prosperous air about it. I explained to the lady custodian about my sponsored walk, and she unhesitatingly allowed me to camp free of charge. With it still being early in the season, I was quite spoiled for choice when it came to picking somewhere to set up my bivouac. Finally I found an ideal spot in the shelter of a small copse of trees and handily convenient for the Gents washroom and toilet. By now I could almost erect the bivouac blindfolded, so in next to no time at all, I was snugly wrapped up in my sleeping bag and sound asleep.

I enjoyed an exotic breakfast the next morning, consisting of three strawberry-flavoured Dextrosol tablets, two packets of curry-flavoured salt peanuts, and a bottle of lucozade. Then I hunted out my tobacco tin to roll a cigarette and enjoy a smoke before I hit the road. Disaster struck. No cigarette papers!

I fully realize that in some people's opinion smoking is both antisocial and extremely unhealthy, but I am afraid I am one of those unfortunate individuals who has been well and truly hooked on the sot-weed since his early teens when it was still quite respectable, and being in the navy, duty free.

I do enjoy my first smoke of the day, and I had all but resigned myself to having to wait until I arrived at the village of East Linton where I could buy some cigarette papers, when my eyes alighted on the only book I carried in my backpack. A copy of the Bible. Friends of mine and people who know me, may be somewhat surprised at my choice of reading material during the walk. But you do not have to be a religious zealot to enjoy this particular book in which there is some excellent stories, a lot of good sense . . . and the thin pages of which make excellent cigarette papers.

... and contemplated the twin sins of blasphemy and sacrilege ...

Lounging back against the base of one of the trees I enjoyed a smoke and contemplated the twin sins of blasphemy and sacrilege. Not because the smouldering tobacco was wrapped in a page torn from a holy book, but because the particular page I was using was the one dedicated to king James I and VI, who was probably one of the earliest members of the anti-smoking lobby.

It was not so much of a day's hard hiking but more of a quiet stroll that morning. With my pushing on to Monksmuir the previous evening, I had travelled a fair bit farther than planned, which left me with only about a dozen miles to walk to my destination for that day at Barns Ness lighthouse near Dunbar.

Once past East Lindon I could look up at the slight eminence of Traprain Law. During Roman times, and for some time after, this grassy hill was the seat of the Votadini tribe, a pro-Roman Celtic people who populated this area of south-east Scotland. Archaeologists claim that the hill once had a population of over 3,000. During excavations back in 1919, a large hoard of Roman silverware was unearthed here.

By midday I had arrived in Dunbar, another old Scottish town which is well steeped in history. 'Toom Tabard', king John Bailiol was soundly defeated in battle here in 1292 by Edward of England. Some 350 years later in 1650 the Scottish army of the Covenant were routed by Oliver Cromwell's New Model Army after foolishly leaving their almost unassailable position on the summit of Doon Hill. The ruins of Dunbar castle are a popular calling place for visitors. It was here that the earl of Bothwell fled with Mary Queen of Scots after the murder of her husband Darnley in 1567. The place held more than historical interest for me though, because Dunbar is the home town of Belhaven beer. This locally brewed beverage is a pint which I would not hesitate to recommend to anybody who has a taste for cask conditioned ales.

It was another hot day but a gentle breeze off the North Sea kept the temperature reasonably pleasant. After sampling a couple of pints of Belhaven, I wandered along the sea shore and across the smooth, green links of Dunbar golf course, heading towards the lighthouse at Barns Ness. The final approach to the tall, slim, white tower of the lighthouse took me through a nature reserve dotted with sand dunes. The sandy path I was following was edged with colourful clumps of yellow-orange kidney vetch, pink thrift, sea milkwort, and the nodding heads of plantains.

Barns Ness lighthouse was built at the turn of the century in 1901. The place has the unfortunate distinction of being the first Scottish lighthouse to be attacked by enemy action in the Second World War, when a homeward bound German aircraft shot the place up in passing with its machine guns. At the time the war was a mere two weeks old. In fact lighthouses became a popular target with the Luftwaffe during the course of the war. Two successive bombing attacks on Fair Isle South lighthouse killed the wives of two of the lightkeepers, and the principal lightkeeper's young daughter. Bell Rock, Pentland Skerries, Stroma and other offshore lighthouses suffered repeated attacks. In fact when I was serving temporarily at Rattray Head lighthouse in 1979, you could still see the wartime scars in the shape of two neat, machine gun bullet holes in the top corner of one of the heavy, glass lenses.

Barns Ness lighthouse courtesy Christopher Nicholson

Barns Ness had been a fully automatic lighthouse for some time before I visited the station. I had been asked to call in here because due to conversion work at the dwelling house at neighbouring St. Abbs Head lighthouse, Barns Ness was being used as the temporary home of the St. Abbs principal lightkeeper Duncan Jordan and his family. Duncan commuted back and forth daily between the two lighthouses.

There was a bothy at Barns Ness, but due to the station having been automated quite some time ago, I discovered that there was no bed in it. However, a couple of rugs and my sleeping bag provided a good enough substitute, and a bellyful of Belhaven, a marvellous soporific.

I was up and away early the next morning for my final day's walking on the east coast leg of my journey. A clammy North Sea haar swirled about the sand dunes making the looming bulk of Torness nuclear power station appear like an unreal, child's model made out of used cardboard cereal packets and the centres of spent toilet rolls, constructed with the aid of a plan from BBC's Blue Peter. Traffic growled and rumbled past me in the murk as I headed cautiously along the A1.

Suddenly, like the lifting of a stage curtain, the haar cleared abruptly to reveal (yes, you have guessed it), a merciless, hot, yellow sun in a burning, blue sky. It was about this time that I had the run in with the two homicidally orientated doberman pinschers which I mentioned earlier.

At the village of Cockburnspath I stopped for a five minute rest and a smoke. I chatted to a lady who was tending her garden next to the public seat upon which I was taking my ease. Here I experienced another example of the 'Jock Tamson syndrome' when I discovered that she came from Wick. She told me that there were several people from Caithness living in the area. They had all been tempted to leave their jobs at Dounreay and move south to work at Torness.

Outside Cockburnspath I left the main artery of the A1 and turned off to follow the steeply climbing secondary road which ran along the flank of a hill called Meickle Black Law. The sun continued to beat down relentlessly as I made this steady ascent, and my clothes were soon clinging to my body with sweat. Although I did not appreciate it at the time, quite nearby was the site of the formidable, coastal stronghold of Fast castle. A fortress long held by the Home family, and regarded as one of the 'keys' of Scotland.

On the approaches to Coldingham moor I came across a stand of trees near the roadside, and I gratefully slumped down in their shade for a breather and a respite from the sun. A short time after setting off on my way again, I was stopped by a local policeman in a patrol car who politely but suspiciously quizzed me as to where was I going and what was I about. I explained to him about my walk, and with a smile and wish of good luck, he slowly drove off. As I headed off across the moor, I thought to myself that the ages old, inbred suspicion of strangers has obviously not died out yet in this part of the borders.

On the outskirts of Coldingham I was stopped by yet another motorist. It wasn't the law this time but Duncan Jordan on his way to stand his watch at St. Abbs Head. We chatted for a few minutes, I virtuously refusing his offer of 'come on and get in the car, no bugger will know', and after I had told him what time I estimated to be at the lighthouse, he drove off. When I arrived in Coldingham village and entered the pub which Duncan had recommended to me, I was pleasantly surprised to find that there was a free pint of beer waiting there for me, courtesy of the principal lightkeeper of St. Abbs Head.

Not far from Coldingham village is Coldingham Priory which was first restored in 1098 in honour of St. Cuthbert by king Edgar of Scotland. In a chequered history the priory was sacked in 1216, burned in 1544, and partially blown up by that arch demolition expert Oliver Cromwell in 1645. Despite all this, the priory is still going strong and is one of the oldest places of continuous worship in the country.

Reluctantly leaving the pleasant little village pub in Coldingham, I followed the serpentine, roller-coaster of a track to St. Abbs Head lighthouse. The road passed through rough grazing land dotted with sheep, and with this area being designated a National Nature Reserve, dotted with tourists of the Barbour jacket and green designer wellies species.

The stubby light-tower at St. Abbs Head was built in 1862, and is perched on top of a high cliff, with the lightkeepers' dwelling houses situated on a slight eminence at the rear. This layout gives the place the peculiarity of being what must be the only lighthouse in Scotland where the lightkeepers have to actually climb down stairs to put the light in at night. On my arrival I found Duncan busily employed in painting the astragals on the tower lantern, and it did seem a bit odd looking down on somebody doing this regular piece of lighthouse maintenance. Seeing me he finished off for the day and ushered me into the radio and watch room where he signed my check-in sheet and thus gained the distinction of being the only lightkeeper to sign for two different lighthouses.

That evening I sat on the bed in the bothy listening to Radio Aberdeen of all things, and feeling an air of quiet satisfaction now that I had successfully negotiated the east coast leg of my walk. My boots still seemed good for another few hundred miles; my bivouac, backpack, and other essential equipment seemed to be standing up well; and I felt fit and raring to tackle what would be the harder part of my journey, the trip up the west coast.

The next morning I arose to face the immediate problem of making my way, by whatever means possible, across country to the Mull of Galloway lighthouse which was to be the starting point for the long and meandering walk up the west coast.

St. Abbs Head lighthouse
courtesy Royal Commission on the Ancient and Historical Monuments of Scotland

The first part of this border interlude was solved when Duncan kindly gave me a lift into Berwick-upon-Tweed, where I knew that I should be able to catch a bus for at least part of the journey. Berwick has probably the bloodiest history of any town in the British Isles. The place was constantly changing hands, usually with the wholesale massacre of the unfortunate inhabitants, in the bitter wars between England and Scotland. The town finally ended up belonging to England, but as every schoolboy will tell you, Berwick boasts the only English football team to play in the Scottish football league. Berwick Rangers were the lowly second division team which back in the sixties shocked the mighty Glasgow Rangers by defeating them one nil and knocking them out of the Scottish cup.

After loitering about Berwick bus terminus for about an hour or so, I managed to catch a bus which took me back across the border through the village of Coldstream and finally deposited me at Kelso. From Kelso the next stage was a bus to Jedburgh, and from there it was another bus to Hawick. This journey was rapidly becoming a guided tour of Scotland's top rugby union clubs. The bus between Jedburgh and Hawick must have covered at least double the actual distance between the two towns as it was a school bus and travelled round and round the border country lanes dropping off schoolchildren at isolated farmhouses.

It almost looked like the end of the line for the day when I eventually arrived at Hawick, because here I discovered that there were no buses going in my direction for several hours. Refusing to give up so early, I decided to hitch-hike, and I took up a stance on the outskirts of the town, resolved that if I had not got a lift by the time the fiftieth vehicle had gone past me, then I would call it a day and find somewhere to bivouac in the Hawick area.

The thirty-seventh motorist, a jazzy little Fiat driven by a gentleman who told me worked as an optical engineer in Hawick, pulled up and gave me a lift as far as Langholm. A sleepy little border town which principally sticks in my mind because of an excellent steeplechaser called the 'Langholm Dyer'.

I had realized at the start of that day that it would be highly unlikely that I should be able to make it to the Mull of Galloway in the one day's travel. In the light of this I had set my target destination for the day as the town of Dumfries where I had an open invitation to stay the night with the daughter of the principal lightkeeper at Holborn Head. Len Fraser was the lightkeeper and his daughter Elma had a Canadian husband Mark. For a while though it looked like it was going to be a matter of either hitch-hiking again or staying overnight in Langholm as it appeared that there were no service buses running until very late that night, but my guardian angel was looking after me still, and I managed to get a seat on a works bus which was bound for Carlisle but stopped off at Gretna on the way.

For the second time that day I crossed the border as the bus headed south for Longtown in Cumbria before turning off and crossing again into Scotland at Gretna. With an ironic smile to myself, I recalled a conversation which I had with a friend of mine some weeks before I had set off on my walk. At the time I had stated that it was over ten years since I had been in England, and here I was visiting the country for the second time in the same day, albeit if only briefly.

Gretna, world famous for its popularity with eloping couples, was quiet and peaceful in the early evening. The tide was out and the Solway Firth, my first glimpse of the western coast, appeared as a long expanse of dirty, grey-yellow sand stretching far into the distance where it merged with the silver ribbon of the sea. Finding a local services timetable in the bus stop where I disembarked, I noted that there would be a bus to Dumfries in three hours. With this time to kill I headed for the nearest pub for something to eat and drink. As soon as I had satisfied the inner man, I 'phoned Elma to tell her that I was on my way but would not be arriving in Dumfries until later that evening. Despite my protests she insisted that Mark would drive through to Gretna and pick me up, which he duly did.

Elma and Mark made me feel very much at home, and we spent the remainder of that evening quietly chatting and drinking Mark's beer. The last time I had seen them both had been at the previous New Year when they had been up at Scrabster staying at Holborn Head lighthouse for the festivities. It had been such a particularly well celebrated New Year that I do not think that any of us remembered too much about it.

I had cause to be grateful that I had a roof over my head and a warm, dry bed to sleep in that night, as early in the morning I was awoken by the sound of torrential rain which was still falling heavily when I arose a couple of hours later. After a filling breakfast, Mark who works for the Forestry Commission, gave me a lift to the Dumfries bus terminal where I could get a bus for Stranraer. Casting a gloomy eye on the weather, I was grateful that this was one of the days on which I would not be doing much walking. As I watched from the bus station, the river Nith seemed to be visibly getting higher with the sheer volume of water that was falling into it from the heavens.

It was an interminably long and boring bus journey in the driving rain. The countryside, partially obscured from sight by the rain streaming bus windows, passed by in a series of washed out greens, greys, and yellows. Wet and bedraggled passengers eagerly leaped on board as the bus stopped at Castle Douglas, Gatehouse of Fleet, Newton Stewart, and practically every small hamlet and village in between. But by the time we had reached Glenluce, the weather had begun to clear, and when we finally arrived in Stranraer, it had turned into a tolerably fair day.

I threaded my way through the busy and bustling Stranraer streets until on seeing a pub advertising bar lunches I decided to stop off for something to eat before attempting to find a bus heading south for the Mull of Galloway. Over a pint in the pub I was fortunate enough to strike up a conversation with a local electrician who informed me that he intended driving down to Drummore that afternoon. This village is situated just a few miles from Mull of Galloway lighthouse, and I willingly accepted his offer of a lift as this would save me quite a long wait in Stranraer before the next bus was due.

I eventually arrived at Mull of Galloway lighthouse by mid-afternoon after having been given a further lift from Drummore by assistant lightkeeper Ron Ireland.

The lighthouse which was built in 1830 stands on a sheer, high headland at the tip of a peninsula of farmland. It was from the summit of this headland that according to legend the Pictish father and son committed suicide by leaping to their deaths rather than give away the secret recipe of Heather ale to the invading Scots. Mull of Galloway was the southernmost extremity of my walk, and is indeed the most southerly point of Scotland.

From the high balcony at the top of the lighthouse it is possible to look to the east and see across the Solway Firth the dark mountains of Cumbria. Looking to the south, the Isle of Man becomes visible and although not part of Scotland, this island also comes under the supervision of the

Mull of Galloway
lighthouse
courtesy of Northern
Lighthouse Board

Northern Lighthouse Board. To the west you can see the coast of Ulster and of course, to the north is Scotland. In years gone by this would have been a view of four kingdoms.

Principal lightkeeper John Lamont greeted me on my arrival and signed my check-in sheet. The bothy was being used by the local lightkeeper that night, but there was a caravan at the station for the use of visitors and the occasional lightkeeper, and in here I would spend the night. Later that evening Ron Ireland and John Lamont invited me to come to the village of Drummore with them where we enjoyed a couple of pints of beer in their local, the Queens Hotel, and also took the opportunity of off-loading another sponsor form for the pub's patrons to subscribe to.

Although it had involved much travelling, and some awkward and unsure travel arrangements, I awoke the following morning to find that my border interlude had quite refreshed me and sharpened my desire to make the assault on the long west coast haul which now lay before me. But before I could begin the long walk north, I had two more lighthouses on the Rhinns of Galloway to visit first, and after demolishing a hearty breakfast cooked by John Lamont, I made my farewells and headed north, bound for Kilantrigan lighthouse situated near the village of Portpatrick on the west coast of the Rhinns.

It was a perfect walking day, dry and neither too hot or too cold. A gentle breeze scudded across Luce Bay filling the brightly coloured spinnaker of a yacht which was tacking across the blue-green waters. I was feeling in a mellow mood which was heightened as I began to appreciate the sentiment behind the expression 'Bonnie Gallowa', as this had to be some of the prettiest countryside which I was to walk through. Not the wild and rugged beauty of the barren northwest, but a more simple, gentle, almost feminine prettiness. Every hedgerow was sprinkled with dog and burnet roses in full bloom. The grassy verges were colourfully splashed with a multitude of wild flowers . . . campions, agrimony, yellow pimpernel, gowans, feverfew, ones I could not identify, and the ever present foxglove. In the damper patches of fields, yellow irises bloomed in profusion, and in other drier parts could be seen a contrast of yellow and red where charlock mingled with poppies. I stopped for a brief rest on a wide, grass covered bank at the side of the road, and on looking down I was delighted to see a sprinkling of delicate, wild pansies at my feet.

My lunchtime stopover for that day was at the village of Sandhead where I enjoyed a pint and a meat pie in the convivial company of the locals who appeared to be carrying on from the previous evening a drinking session of almost suicidal proportions. Not wishing to become involved I did not stay long but headed off down the narrow country lane which would take me across to the western coast of the Rhinns and the road for Portpatrick.

The fields which I was now passing were almost all full of healthy looking cattle quietly grazing on the lush, green grass. I recognized several popular breeds and cross-breeds of cattle, but I felt a little bit disappointed that I failed to see any of the distinctively white banded Belted Galloways.

The narrow country lane eventually joined up with the main Stranraer-Portpatrick road on the outskirts of Portpatrick. I took an immediate liking to this scenically beautiful little village. The rocky harbour was jam-packed with visiting yachts and motor launches, over for the day from nearby Ulster. In fact there were so many broad, twanging Ulster accents to be heard on the seafront, that a stranger might be forgiven if he thought himself in Port Rush rather than Portpatrick. This is not surprising as up until 1862, Portpatrick was the principal ferry terminal for the crossing to Northern Ireland. Ferries from here regularly completed the 21 mile crossing to Donaghadee in Ulster.

I had a further two miles to walk along the coast to Kilantrigan lighthouse, but having been completely seduced by Portpatrick, and having some time on my hands, I resolved to linger there awhile. I 'phoned up Kilantrigan principal lightkeeper Louis Hendry to tell him of my plans, and that I would not be arriving until some time that evening. Louis replied that was fine by him, and as I was in the town, would I mind looking up a cousin of his who worked with the local ladies lifeboat guild and was keen to meet me.

Mrs. Patsy Milligan was Louis's cousin, and I tracked her down in the local lifeboat shed where she was presiding over the souvenir stall which was set amidst an exhibition in the shed about the local boat and the RNLI in general.

In conversation with a couple of the town's locals later that day, I found out that Patsy's efforts with the exhibition and souvenir stall, had raised literally thousands of pounds for the RNLI. Ladies like Patsy are the unsung heroines of the lifeboat service, turning out and giving their time and effort in organizing coffee mornings, selling raffle tickets, running flag days, and dozens of different fund raising enterprises which have enabled Britain to have and maintain a lifeboat service without any financial assistance from the government. It is a lifeboat service which is the envy of Europe, if not the world. I hope I do not sound patronising, but as an ex-seaman it comes straight from the heart when I say they do a grand job.

I spent some time chatting to Patsy and looking around the exhibition. As I was about to leave she instructed me to call in across the road at the Crown Hotel where I was to have a meal on behalf of the local lifeboat guild. This was a kind and much appreciated gesture. The Crown was owned by an ex-coxswain of the Portpatrick lifeboat, and the food was excellent.

After my meal I lingered about the sea front for a while, enjoying the sights and sounds of the harbour. Finally I reluctantly headed off along the road which would take me to Kilantrigan lighthouse. As I discovered later, this was an unnecessary long journey. There was a public footpath along the clifftop which led to the lighthouse and which if I had taken would have saved me at least a mile walk.

This particular lighthouse was built in 1900, and I believe that the odd, onomatopoeic name of 'Kilantrigan' means the church of St. Kentigern. St. Kentigern was the renowned Celtic saint who under the name of St. Mungo is revered as the patron saint of the city of Glasgow. In other parts of the country, particularly Cumbria, he is known as St. Trinian. I wonder what the venerable, old holyman would have thought of the young ladies who in the popular series of movies attended the school dedicated to him.

Leaving the main road I joined a single track by-way which led through farm grazing land up to the lighthouse on the cliff-girt coastline. At the

Kilantrigan
courtesy of Northern Lighthouse Board

turn off to this track I stopped to open a cattle grid gate for a pretty, young woman out hacking on a handsome, Highland pony. She rode alongside of me for some distance, and told me that she was married to the local farmer. With my fondness for the animals, the conversation naturally came around to horses. Our talk was interrupted every so often as I opened and closed what seemed to be an endless succession of cattle grid gates. This was a chore I did not in the least mind performing, as I well recalled when I owned my own horse up in Shetland, what a bind it could be continually mounting and dismounting to open these gates.

On my eventual arrival at the lighthouse, principal lightkeeper Louis Hendry welcomed me, and after signing my check-in sheet he invited me up to his house for a chat over a couple of drams. The only time I had met Louis in the past was for a fleeting couple of minutes on the wave lashed Bell Rock lighthouse landing. Louis had been going ashore for a union meeting in Edinburgh, and I had been sent out to the Bell to take his place. We found that we did have quite a few acquaintances in common, and it was quite late before I headed off to my bed in the bothy.

It was a clammy humid kind of night and I had trouble sleeping, which is unusual for me. I found that it was too warm to sleep in the sleeping bag, and too cold to sleep on top of it. I eventually compromised by rooting about the bothy and finding a counterpane to cover me which seemed to achieve the right temperature.

After my uncomfortable night I did not exactly feel too fresh the following morning. I quit the bothy and spent ten minutes taking a couple of photographs of the lighthouse. Then hoisting my backpack on to my back, I headed back along the road and its numerous cattle grids, making my way to the main road and the day's journey to the last lighthouse on the Rhinns of Galloway, the lighthouse at Corsewall situated at the extreme north-west tip of the Rhinns.

By the time I had reached the main road a light drizzle had started up which coated everything with a silvery-grey sheen of moisture and made me put on my waterproofs which were uncomfortable to walk in as despite the drizzle, the day was clammily warm. To cheer myself up I listened to Radio Ulster on my backpack transistor radio, the only sound to intrude on the quiet road. I found that when I was in the south west of Scotland, most of the time I could obtain far better reception of Radio Ulster than Radio Scotland. I also noticed that most people had their televisions tuned in to Ulster television.

The road twisted and turned past rain dripping woodland, slightly cheered up by the brilliant splashes of colour provided by the rhododendron bushes bordering the road at Lochnaw castle.

A little after midday I arrived at the village of Leswalt where a sad-eyed, old man informed me at my enquiry that there was no pub in the village and the nearest one was at Kirkcolm, a couple of miles away.

. . . there was no pub in the village . . .

The grey murk of the morning slowly cleared to reveal blue skies which were mirrored in the still waters of Loch Connell which I passed just before entering the village of Kirkcolm. It was a typical Sunday scene in the village; the churchgoers were returning from Church, the indifferent queued at the newsagents for Sunday papers and the ungodly were enjoying a dinner time pint at the local pub. I joined the ranks of the latter by entering the public bar of the Blue Peter Inn, wondering facetiously when I noticed the pub's name, how many pints I would have to drink before I qualified for a badge. I eventually had a couple to help replace the moisture I had lost through sweating in my waterproofs all morning. After three packets of peanuts and a quick browse through a Sunday paper which someone had discarded on the table near where I was sitting, I left for the last few miles to Corsewall point.

The road followed the shore of Loch Ryan for a time, and I passed the inlet known as the 'Wig'. This place had during the First and Second World Wars been an important base for sea-planes and flying boats. I tried to visualize the lumbering Sunderlands and Catalinas taking off from the choppy waters of the loch. It must have been an impressive sight to behold at the time.

Leaving the lochside the road passed briefly through woodland and then into the ever present, fertile farmlands of Galloway, before petering off at the rocky point of land where the gleaming white tower of Corsewall lighthouse dominated the coastline. This lighthouse came into being in the year 1816 when it was built to light the approaches to the Firth of Clyde. Corsewall Point is a fully manned lighthouse and acts as the control radio station for the other Clyde approaches lighthouses of Ailsa Craig, Sanda and Pladda.

Word had got around the Galloway grapevine that I was due to arrive at Corsewall some time that afternoon, and I was greeted by Andy the occasional lightkeeper who was on duty, and had been keeping an eye out for me. Andy ushered me into the bothy, which I was to share with him that night. He was also kind enough to share his tea with me which was more than welcome as I had eaten nothing but the packets of peanuts in the Blue Peter in Kirkcolm that day.

About an hour after tea we were visited in the bothy by Corsewall's principal lightkeeper Hector Lamont, who is a brother of John the principal at the Mull of Galloway. One more Lamont brother makes up the trio who are all principal lightkeepers, and that is Murdoch who is stationed at Neist Point lighthouse on the island of Skye.

Hector had been away from the station when I had arrived that afternoon, and he was calling over at the bothy to say hello and invite me up to his house for a drink with him and his wife, his sister-in-law and her husband who were down on holiday. It turned into a super evening. Hector's wife Esther, and her sister Margaret both came originally from Scarfskerry in Caithness, and we discovered that we had many friends in common. The whisky flowed quite freely and so did the conversation. It was quite late before I headed off to the bothy and bed, with Hector demanding that I call around in the morning for my breakfast before I started off on my day's walk.

Breakfast the following morning turned out to be a highly comical affair. Hector asked me if his brother John had given me a good feed before I had set off from the Mull of Galloway. I replied that John had cooked an excellent plate of bacon and eggs for me. On hearing this reply Hector uttered a non-committal grunt, and disappeared off into the kitchen. He emerged a few minutes later bearing a plate brimming with food which he laid down in front of me and commenced to point out the various fried delicacies with such comments as: "I bet brother John never gave you fried tomatoes, eh? What about sausages? . . . I bet you never got sausages!"

I could barely eat my breakfast for laughing at these antics, and I solemnly promised that should I happen to meet Murdoch when I passed through the island of Skye, I would certainly see if I could persuade him to cook me a breakfast so I could compare it with his brothers' efforts.

As I previously mentioned in the early stages of my walk, after Dunnet Head I had resolved never to walk the same road twice, unless I had no option. The trip into Stranraer that morning would have meant retracing my steps of the previous day, so I accepted a lift from Andy the occasional lightkeeper, who was heading home to Stranraer that morning, his part-time duties over for the time being.

Andy dropped me off in the centre of the town, and I headed off into a stiff north-westerly wind which was causing quite a chop on Loch Ryan which bordered the road I was following. Looking down the loch I could see an Ulster bound ferry nosing its way out of Cairn Ryan. I wondered how many of the passengers would be foregoing their dinner today.

The traffic became heavy as I rounded the curve of the loch and began to walk northwards. The majority of the vehicles appeared to be heavy goods lorries heading for the Irish ferry terminals at Stranraer or Cairn Ryan. I found it quite prudent to give these mini-juggernauts as wide a berth as possible as they trundled past me. Looking out across the loch at the opposite shore, I could clearly see the road on which I had been walking on the previous day, running parallel with the one which I now followed in the opposite direction. This was a vaguely annoying situation which I was to encounter many times on the much indented and sea loch ridden west coast.

The village of Cairn Ryan passed in a straggle of brightly coloured houses looking down on the bustle of the ferry terminal. During the Second World War this port had been one of the principal landing places for the battered survivors of the Atlantic convoys ravaged by U-boats. The road out of the village began to twist and climb away from the lochside, taking me through the thickly wooded countryside of Glen App. After a while the trees thinned out and I could look down upon the silver thread of the water of App as it traced its way along the glen bottom to the sea. Wooden signs which were either genuinely crudely constructed, or meant to represent rustic simplicity, advertised fresh and smoked salmon.

After a fairly mundane afternoon's hike, I approached the bridge which would take me over the 'romantically' named river Stinchar, and into the sleepy little seaside town of Ballantrae which was my target destination for the day. The earlier strong winds had dropped and the early evening was calm and peaceful. For some minutes I idly leaned against the parapet of the bridge and watched a handful of anglers going through the dexterous, almost ballet-like motions of experienced fly fishermen.

For some reason the name Ballantrae seemed to sound to me like the archetypal name of a Scottish village. The sort of thing that might be dreamed up by a writer of romances or a Hollywood director, like the name Brigadoon. In fact the name derives directly from the Gaelic Baile-an-Traigh, which translated into English simply means 'the village on the shore'. Ballantrae is a quiet little town with some connections with the fishing industry, although things must have been different a couple of hundred years ago when the place was renowned as a hotbed of smuggling activities.

Less than a hundred yards from the bridge I found a pub where I called in for a pint and something to eat prior to finding somewhere to put up my bivouac for the night. The patrons of the bar recommended that I erect my bivouac on the beach, telling me that people often camped there, unbothered by the authorities as it was common land. I thanked them for this information, and after finishing my pint, I headed off towards the sea-shore.

As I walked through the village I recognized the name of one of the streets as being the street where retired principal lightkeeper Bill Frazer lived. Bill had been a bit of a character when he was in the job, and the keepers at Mull of Galloway and Corsewall had urged me to drop in and visit him when they had heard that I might be stopping off at Ballantrae. I did not personally know the man, and this had made me a bit reluctant to go out of my way just to pay a call in passing. But now that I had time to kill, and finding myself in the relevant street, I decided to drop in and give him my regards before I put up my bivouac on the beach for the night.

I am glad that I called, as once introductions had been made, Bill invited me into his house and provided me with an excellent evening's entertainment. He refused to hear of me camping out, and insisted that I made use of his spare bedroom for the night.

Although Bill had lived in Scotland almost all of his days, he still retained his native Ulster accent, and no shortage of Irish wit. He kept me laughing with his tales until well after midnight that night, and I could have willingly stayed up longer as this man was a born raconteur.

Despite my late night, I arose fairly early the following morning. I said farewell and thanks to Bill, promising faithfully that I would drop in and see him should I ever find myself down that part of the country again. I set off at a brisk pace, hoping to be in Girvan by midday when I had a meeting to attend with the people involved with the Girvan lifeboat. The northwest wind which I had thought had blown itself out the previous day, had started again with renewed strength, but otherwise the day was fair with clear blue skies up above. The road ran parallel to the sandy shoreline which I thought was spoiled by the appearance every few hundred yards of large wooden signs which stated 'Private. No Camping'. Signs such as these, and the even more common 'Private. No Fishing', and 'Private. No Trespassers', were far too prevalent along the entire length of the west coast. I am afraid that the sight of such notices tend to bring out the latent anarchist in me, and had I been carrying an axe in my backpack, I think that I would have had quite a considerable supply of kindling by the time I reached Cape Wrath.

Dominating the skyline to seaward along that coast, is the bulk of Ailsa Craig, which the poet Keats described as a 'craggy pyramid', and the local Ayr folk christened 'Paddy's milestone'. Ailsa Craig granite was once in great demand for the manufacture of curling stones. Lightkeepers who have served at the lighthouse there, have shown me photographs of the old quarries where this industry used to be carried out. In places you can see strange, smooth, bowl-like depressions in the rock, indicating where the stonemasons had carved out individual curling stones.

At Lendalfoot I looked up to see if I could see Carelton castle which according to the old Scottish ballad was the home of Sir John who had a nice little business going in marrying wealthy women and then throwing them off the nearby cliff-top. The song says that he got away with this nefarious ploy seven times in succession, but unfortunately for Sir John the eighth bride turned the tables and threw him over the cliff.

Not too far from Lendalfoot I walked through the narrow Kennedy's Pass which is flanked by steep rock. This was Carrick, and clan Kennedy country which was of particular interest to me as my surname of Cassells is a mis-spelling of the Kennedy family name of Cassillis (incidentally, both are pronounced the same way, as in the word 'castles'). Back in the 1500s a bloody and bitter feud developed between the Cassillis branch of clan Kennedy and the Barganey branch of the clan. This conflict lasted for decades, until the very last surviving member of the Barganey faction was stabbed to death in Edinburgh by two Cassillis supporters.

I arrived in the pleasant little seaside town of Girvan with enough time on hand to demolish a large helping of fish and chips before I headed for the local lifeboat shed where I had arranged to meet Mrs. Vi Bone and members of the local ladies lifeboat guild. Waiting for me at the shed was Mike Storey, coxswain of the Girvan boat. Mike and I chatted away about Girvan and about my walk, and we were soon joined by Mary Davidson, president of the Girvan ladies lifeboat guild, Vi Bone, secretary of the guild, and a member of the 'Young Vauxs', Girvan's junior lifeboat supporters. Mrs. Bone being a very astute lady, presented me with a couple of tins of beer, which washed the fish and chips down a treat. We all duly posed for photographs for the local papers, with the Girvan lifeboat in the background. Another short chat, and then I wished everybody goodbye and I set off with the hope of reaching Turnberry lighthouse by evening.

Much of that afternoon was spent walking past fields full of new potatoes. The light green of the sprouting tattie shaws contrasting nicely with the light reddish-yellow of the fertile Ayrshire soil. Due to the dry weather of the past few weeks, several fields had sprinklers operating in them. One farmer had situated one of his sprinklers too near to the edge of the field, and every few seconds a cool silver shower cascaded over the passing traffic, the sun causing a miniature rainbow to flicker momentarily in the errant spray.

By early evening I was trudging past the famous links of Turnberry golf course. The whole place was a hive of bustling activity as workmen in a variety of different coloured overalls, swept things, painted things, pulled things, pushed things, and erected tents and scaffolding for the spectator stands and television camera positions. This activity was all for the benefit of the Turnberry Open which was due to take place the following week.

I could not fail to notice the official pennants of the tournament; these small triangular flags seemed to be fluttering all over the place and represented a white lighthouse on a blue background. I thought that this was quite appropriate as Turnberry lighthouse is situated on the golf course itself. One of the holes is called the 'lighthouse hole' and the access road to the lighthouse cuts right across the course. It goes without saying that Turnberry lighthouse has long been a popular posting with those lighthouse keepers who are also keen golfers. This posting is made all the more attractive as the Turnberry golf club's policy is to make the lightkeepers honorary members of the club.

Turning off the main road, I walked along the lighthouse access road. I passed the greens and fairways where very shortly the likes of Seve Ballesteros, Greg Norman, and our own Sam Torrance would be fighting it out.

Turnberry lighthouse was built in 1863, reputedly on the site of the ruins of Turnberry castle which was once the home of the Countess of Carrick, who was Robert the Bruce's mum. This lighthouse is now fully automatic but I had been requested to call in here as the place was now used as the on-shore accommodation for two of the six Ailsa Craig lightkeepers. Coincidentally, the two keepers living there at the time, although not related to each other, were both called Norman Douglas.

The Norman Douglas who happened to be ashore at the time, welcomed me on arrival and ushered me into his house for a cup of coffee. Norman is a keen golfer and with the Turnberry Open coinciding with his four weeks ashore from Ailsa Craig, he was at that time, probably the

Turnberry lighthouse
courtesy of Christopher Nicholson

happiest man in the entire lighthouse service. In fact a short time after my visit, I read in the papers that an American golf fan had offered Norman several thousand pounds plus a free holiday of their choice for his family, if he would agree to let his house to the American for the duration of the Open.

Norman, his wife Pauline, and daughters Leslie and Karen, made me feel very welcome. As Pauline put the girls off to bed, Norman and I had a good long chat over a couple of tins of beer. We talked about the walk, mutual friends, horse racing — and I was pleased to find that I had met somebody else just as daft about this particular sport as I was — and inevitably golf. Now I am not a golf fan, and I flippantly commented that I had always regarded the game as a trivial way of spoiling a perfectly good walk, or a game played by men with small balls. At these remarks, my host favoured me with the sort of look a devout Christian missionary would have bestowed on a particularly recalcitrant heathen.

After we had finished the beer, Norman considerately offered me the use of his washing machine and tumble drier. This offer I gratefully accepted as my stock of clean clothes was virtually non-existent at the time, and I had been planning on searching out a laundromat when I arrived in Ayr the next day.

There was a sequel to my laundry session that night. Although I did not realize it at the time, I had lost a pair of underpants in the wash. A week after I had successfully completed the walk and had returned to my home in Scrabster, I received in the post a package containing the missing garment, with an enclosed letter which stated: 'Found these jammed in the tumble drier after you had left. I think they must be yours. A most unusual calling card. Regards. Norman Douglas.'

Pauline kindly cooked breakfast for me before I set off for Ayr the next morning. The skies were overcast and there was a threat of rain in the air as I retraced my steps across the golf course and followed the main road down through the village of Maidens. I stopped for my first five minute break of the day, and a chance to consult my road map, in a lay-by next to the wooded grounds of Culzean castle. This magnificent castle was constructed between 1772 and 1792 by the architect Robert Adam for the Marquis of Ailsa Craig, chief of clan Kennedy. The place is now owned by the National Trust, and the castle with its beautiful gardens are very popular with the tourists, particularly Americans, due to General Eisenhower's close association with Culzean during the Second World War.

Looking at my map I found that I had a choice of two roads, both of the same length, which would take me to Ayr. The main road was the coastal route which crossed the strange phenomenon known as the 'Electric Brae', an optical illusion which convinces you that you are going up hill when you are actually going down. The other road was marked on my map as a secondary road and ran further inland through a couple of small villages. I had travelled on the coastal route over the Electric Brae several times in the past when I had been visiting this area, but the B road was virgin territory to me. For this reason, and the fact that it was a B road and would therefore presumably have less traffic travelling along it, decided me.

As I had predicted, the traffic was thankfully light on this road. My only complaint was of the monotony of the featureless farmlands which I found myself passing through on the afternoon's walk. A landscape without a great deal of character. Even the small villages which I passed through seemed sad and grey under the overcast sky.

The day's ever present threat of rain came good as I entered Alloway on the outskirts of the city of Ayr itself. I began to notice signposts indicating the route of the Burns Heritage Trail. It was in Alloway where the 'auld haunted kirk' of Tam O'Shanter fame was situated. I walked past Burns' cottage where soggy tourists were jostling one another to have their photographs taken as they shivered alongside the simple, white-washed, rain-streaming walls. Looking on the scene, with the eager photographers wearing their hastily donned, multi-coloured kagouls, and flashing away

... the scene ... would have tickled the bard's irascible sense of humour ...

with their expensive Minoltas, Leicas and Yashikas, I thought that the scene provided a situation which I am sure would have tickled the bard's irascible sense of humour.

'Auld Ayr that ne'er a toon surpasses, for honest men and bonny lassies', wrote Rabbie. I can certainly vouch for the latter part of this sentiment as I passed some smashers on my way into the city centre. It was only mid-afternoon and I had intended pushing on to Troon and getting in touch with the local lifeboat people there, but for some unknown reason while I was walking through the busy city streets I began to feel light-headed and distinctly peculiar. What I think the Victorian ladies used to term 'a touch of the vapours'. I entered a nearby pub and to my relief a seat and a pint of beer seemed to do the trick as well as any Victorian lady's quick whiff of the sal volatile, and the sudden affliction went as quickly as it had come. However, just to be on the safe side, I decided to go no further that day but to find somewhere in Ayr to stay bed and breakfast for the night.

Ayr has long been one of my favourite Scottish towns and is a place which holds many mixed memories for me. When I was a child, my parents took my brother and myself on some marvellous holidays at the nearby Butlins holiday camp and my late wife had been a student of agriculture at nearby Auchincruve college when I first married her. In fact due to the circumstances at the time, we spent our honeymoon in Ayr. Hilary was the treasurer of the college's student union and had to be present at Auchincruve for the annual audit the week after our wedding. She spent two days poring over the union's accounts, while I enjoyed two days at the Ayr racecourse October meeting.

We were married just before Hilary started her final year at college. At the time I was working at Dounreay, and on those weekends when she could not travel north to Caithness where we had our home, I would head south to be with her. The problem of finding somewhere to stay on my occasional trips to Ayr often provided some comical moments. One particular weekend I found myself as the only male resident of Craigie college ladies halls of residence. Hilary was staying in the halls of residence at the time, and due to our marital status, the authorities allowed me to stay the weekend with her. Being the only male in the living quarters of dozens of young and pretty female students was an experience which I will not forget in a long time. It certainly was an interesting and educational weekend.

It was not to be the ladies hall of residence this time though, and I found digs for the night at the Fialte guesthouse owned by a smashing couple called Mr. and Mrs. Thompson. Bill Thompson, a Telecom worker when he was not playing mine host at the Fialte, had heard about my walk, and insisted on calling the local radio station with the news that I had arrived in town. Radio West asked if I minded coming around to their studios for a short interview. The next thing I knew, I was being whisked through the town in Bill's car, and was soon being recorded for a quick five minute spot, by an extremely attractive lady presenter.

That evening, after a hot bath and a change of clothes, I had a good wander about the town. This walk evoked many memories, most of them happy ones, and I do believe that if there had been a race meeting the next day at Ayr racecourse, I do not think that I could have summoned up the same fortitude which enabled me to walk past the Musselburgh racecourse.

Just prior to my leaving on the following morning, I asked for my bill to settle up for my night's stay. To my pleasant surprise I found that a very generous discount had been made by the Thompsons as their donation towards the walk.

I started off slightly later than usual that morning, as I had to visit the bank. I found a branch of the bank which I use in Prestwick, as I was passing through on my way northwards. Robert the Bruce was a regular visitor to the Prestwick area in days gone by — not to make use of its banking facilities but to visit a holy well which was situated here, and where he would take the waters in an attempt to find relief from the leprosy which afflicted him in his later years.

The rain of the previous day had cleared and the sun was shining brightly once more. Jet aircraft screeched overhead, landing and taking off from Prestwick airport. One particular jet passed so low over my head that

I felt I could jump up in the air and grab hold of its undercarriage. There was quite a lot of road traffic as well as air traffic, but the verges at the side of the road were a good ten or twelve yards wide, and the grass was cropped short enough to make walking on them comfortable.

The road by-passed Troon where I had originally planned to stay the previous evening. I found out, long after my walk, that the name Troon is not, as I thought, derived from the Gaelic, but from the Ancient British word 'Trwyn', which in English means 'nose'. This is well understood if you look at a map of this part of the coast and you can see that the point of land on which Troon is situated does indeed look like an outsized, slightly Roman hooter, sniffing inquisitively into the Firth of Clyde.

At Drybridge on the outskirts of Irvine, I came across one of these 'pick your own' farming enterprises, next to the road. A number of families were quite industriously engaged in filling straw baskets with gooseberries and strawberries. I stopped and watched them for a while, and wondered to myself how much the owners of such a place had to write off in fruit nibbled by the pickers while they picked. I saw one trio of wee bairns descend on a row of strawberry plants with all the voracity and appetite of a swarm of hungry locusts.

Back in the 18th century, before the river Clyde was dredged and deepened, Irvine was the principal port for Glasgow. However, much of the place is now what is termed a 'new town'. I almost got lost walking through Irvine, but this did not surprise me unduly. There is a saying that a camel is really a horse designed by a committee. I am certain that the same committee designs new towns. After coming to a dead end twice and being forced to retrace my steps, I eventually managed to extricate myself from the place. The one thing that particularly sticks in my mind about the predicament I found myself in, was that I never met one pedestrian who I could ask for directions. The entire population of Irvine seemed to be going about their business in cars.

Having regained the main road I followed the coast. The day had become warm and humid as I by-passed Stevenston, and the traffic was passing by slowly, nose to tail. Eventually I arrived in Saltcoats which I walked through to the neighbouring town of Ardrossan, my destination for the day.

Ardrossan was created and planned by the Earl of Eglinton in 1805. The earl's name is perpetuated in the Eglinton Hotel, owned by the singer Calum Kennedy. My funds were looking pretty healthy after my visit to the bank in Prestwick, and it seemed unlikely that I would find anywhere to camp in the immediate vicinity of the town, so I opted to spend another night in bed and breakfast lodgings. As it turned out, this was to be the last time I was to make use of this type of accommodation. Totalling things up afterwards, I found that I had only used bed and breakfast facilities on six occasions during the entire walk. This was far fewer times than I had privately predicted to myself before setting off.

To pass the time that evening I went out for a pint in down-town Ardrossan. I ended up in the bar of the Eglinton Hotel, and although I did not meet Calum, I chatted for a while with his charming wife who was presiding behind the bar.

Another 'Jock Tamson syndrome' incident cropped up that night. The only other occupants of the bar turned out to be two Orcadians from the island of Shapinsay. Being fellow northerners, we soon got talking. When I asked them what they were doing in this neck of the woods, so far from home they told me that they were crewing a coaster which was lying up for the night in Ardrossan harbour. On exchanging names, I discovered that I knew the father of one of the Orkney men, having last seen him when he was at the fishing. His son told me that his dad was no longer at the fishing but was in fact the skipper of the coaster. We had a couple of drinks, and they suggested that if I fancied hanging around Ardrossan for a couple of days, they would pick me up and give me a lift to Campbelltown on their return trip south. If they had been going to Campbelltown the next day, it would have been very tempting to accept, but as things stood, I declined their offer. The fact that I had suddenly remembered that the last fishing boat of which the father had been skipper, had sunk a mile or so south of Sumburgh Head in Shetland a few years previously, had nothing at all to do with my refusal.

Before returning for the night to my boarding house, I made some enquiries about the departure times of the ferry for Arran which I intended catching in the morning. When I had initially plotted out my route around the mainland lighthouses, it had immediately become apparent to me that quite a good deal of unnecessary mileage could be saved on the west coast route, by the occasional island hopping. So the next day I intended sailing to Brodick on the island of Arran, then taking a bus to Lochranza from where I could catch another ferry to Claonig on the Kintyre peninsula. From Claonig I hoped to walk to Campbelltown, which would be quite a long hike for one day, but I felt up to it.

The Northwest passage home . . .

Rain; island hopping; midges and more bloody rain!

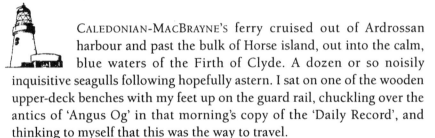

CALEDONIAN-MACBRAYNE'S ferry cruised out of Ardrossan harbour and past the bulk of Horse island, out into the calm, blue waters of the Firth of Clyde. A dozen or so noisily inquisitive seagulls following hopefully astern. I sat on one of the wooden upper-deck benches with my feet up on the guard rail, chuckling over the antics of 'Angus Og' in that morning's copy of the 'Daily Record', and thinking to myself that this was the way to travel.

With the newspaper still lying open on my lap, I dozed off, lulled by the combination of the fresh sea air, the gentle motion of the ferry, and the warm, summer sunshine. I did not wake up until the ferry berthed with a slight bump alongside the jetty at Brodick. I watched the gangway being slowly lowered into position which was immediately followed by the speedy evacuation of my fellow passengers, most of them heading directly for nearby Brodick castle and its colourful, flower-filled gardens. This castle was a former stronghold of the Hamilton clan who were the rulers of Arran from 1503 until 1895.

I headed for the Lochranza bus where I almost became involved in a heated altercation with the driver, but decided that discretion was the better part of valour when I realized that this was the only bus heading my way for quite some time. Anyway, the poor chap was suffering severe harassment from a large, miscellaneous party of foreign tourists.

Once we were all finally settled on board the bus, we were driven off along a road which was so narrow and negotiated so many sudden and blind corners, that before we had travelled two miles I was beginning to fully sympathize with the driver's foul temper.

I had noticed that lately I was beginning to encounter more and more fellow backpackers, a fact which I put down to the 'get-away-from-it-all' beauty of the west coast and islands and by now the holiday season was in full swing. The variety of packs and loads being carried often caused me a bit of amusement. From the comfort of my bus seat I watched a party of six, loaded down like Sherpas and looking for all the world like an advance party on the lower slopes of Everest, but in reality attempting to negotiate the lower slopes of the 2,867 feet high Goat Fell. What they were planning on doing with the vast amount of equipment which they were straining to carry on up to the summit, was quite beyond me.

Another backpacking incident which raised a smile, was a sight which I saw in Oban. It consisted of a large, well-built man with a rucksack which was so small it could have only carried a change of socks and underwear. But walking just behind him was his companion, a slim, petite lady who appeared even shorter than her probable four feet ten, because she was bent almost double under the weight of one of the largest backpacks I have ever seen. It was topped with a rolled up tent and had a variety of pots, pans and miscellaneous articles dangling by string from the bulging sides.

. . . a sight which I saw in Oban . . .

But, back to Arran, where after a journey of many stops, the bus finally pulled into Lochranza. Here I disembarked and favoured the driver with a smile which I am afraid was probably something of a cross between a leer and a snarl. He duly growled back in reply.

Back in the boom days of the herring fishing, Lochranza was one of the more important ports around these parts. The horseshoe of surrounding hills provided a naturally sheltered harbour and anchorage for the herring fishing fleets of the south-west coast.

I strolled along to consult the timetable at the head of the ferry jetty. Finding that I had nearly two hours to wait before the next boat to Claonig, I popped into the nearby Lochranza Hotel for a pint and a sandwich. The price of the beer here was the most expensive that I had so far encountered, and was only to be beaten by the price charged in a certain hotel in Oban. Incidentally the cheapest pint I bought was in Haddington. I did not really begrudge paying over the odds for a pint of beer in a place like Lochranza which has to rely heavily on the few summer months of the tourist trade, but I regarded the price charged in Oban as a pure and simple rip-off.

The ferry duly arrived on time, and after a short and uneventful trip across Kilbrannan Sound, I landed on the Kintyre peninsula at Claonig. Claonig isn't so much a place, but rather just the name of the particular spot of countryside on the peninsula, where the ferry lands. As I strode out for the long hike to Campbeltown, I could hear behind me the handful of bemused tourists who had landed off the ferry with me, muttering among themselves about where were the shops, and was there a restaurant here?

I strode off along the narrow, roller coaster of a road passing alternately sun-dappled wooded patches and then through rough open heath where black-faced sheep grazed. This being the secondary of the two roads which run the length of the Kintyre peninsula, there was not a great deal of traffic, and what there was, almost exclusively tourist. I was making pretty good time and beginning to feel quite optimistic about making it in one push to Campbeltown. I had decided that if this walk began to look impossible in the one go, I would stop and bivouac for the night at Carradale. It must have been the invigorating effects of the fresh sea air and the ease of my rest on the ferry crossing that morning from Ardrossan, but when I arrived at Carradale I still felt fighting fit and full of walking, and after a brief five minute rest, I put aside all thoughts of camping there the night and headed south, absolutely determined to reach Campbeltown that day or bust.

The weather held good, the slowly setting sun lengthening the shadows of the trees around the ruins of Saddell Abbey. This place was once regarded as religiously important a site as Iona. A few miles past the abbey, feeling tired, leg-weary, but very self-satisfied with myself, I arrived in Campbeltown. It was about nine o-clock in the evening and I was utterly famished. Catching the appetizing smell of a fish and chip shop, I followed my nose, and some twenty minutes later I had quite unashamedly devoured two large fish and chip suppers, one after the other.

I have for many years been a great fan of the Scottish author Neil Munro, and in particular his hilariously funny book *The Tales of the Vital Spark*, the collection of short stores about the Clyde puffer and the various antics of Captain Para Handy and the rest of the crew. Well I was now well and truly in 'Vital Spark' country, and when I saw a bar called the 'Para Handy', I just had to drop in there for a drink to wash down the fish suppers.

As it was a Friday night, the pub was quite crowded and I soon fell in with a gang of local worthies who provided excellent entertainment. They quizzed me about my backpack, and when I told them about my walk, I was kindly offered several invitations for a bed for the night. I was feeling dog-tired and not at all looking forward to finding somewhere to pitch my bivouac so late at night, I gratefully accepted one of these offers.

Feeling just a bit thick headed, and with a slight ache in my leg muscles, I awoke the next morning on the couch where I had slept the night. My host was sitting at a nearby table enjoying his breakfast which seemed to consist of a bottle of cheap wine and a tin of lager. I politely declined his offer to join him, and after a quick cup of coffee and a cigarette, I thanked him for the hospitality and took to the road once more for the walk to the Mull of Kintyre lighthouse.

Campbeltown, or Kilkerran as it used to be called before the Campbell clan appropriated the bulk of the Kintyre peninsula, was just coming to life for the day as I trudged through the streets.

Out in Campbeltown loch — the loch which the Scottish singer Andy Stewart wished was whisky and if it was, from what I saw of the regulars in the Para Handy bar the night before, it would not have lasted long — I could see the looming bulk of Davarr island. This island can be reached on foot at low tide, and at one time I had been toying with the idea of visiting Davarr lighthouse. Unfortunately however, this lighthouse, like so many others, had recently been made fully automatic and completely demanned.

I followed the road south through the beautiful, if rugged, countryside celebrated in song by Paul McCartney. A terrible song, but that is just a personal opinion, it was certainly popular enough at the time of its release. The famous ex-Beatle, singer and songwriter lived around these parts, but I never did discover exactly which of the scattered farms and houses was chez McCartney.

From the heights above Carskey Bay my natural cynicism left me for a short while and I full realized how someone could be so moved to write a song, however trite I thought it, about this part of the country. It was a sunny day with that kind of pristinely clear visibility you sometimes get after heavy rain, as if the sky has had an eye-wash. The sea was calm and coloured a deep aquamarine blue, fringed with a ragged, pure white border where the waves lapped onto the golden sands of a deserted beach. A small flotilla of yachts, their gaily coloured spinnakers bellying in the moderate breeze, sailed out of sight around the emerald green island of Sanda. Just hidden from my sight, somewhere below me, I knew was situated the village of Southend where traditionally St. Columbus first landed on the Scottish mainland from Ireland on his mission to convert the heathen Picts in about AD 560. Ireland itself appeared as a faded green band fifteen miles distant over the sea.

The narrow single track road which would eventually lead me to the lighthouse, was, with the exception of the occasional black-faced sheep, completely deserted. Judging by the numerous patches of couch grass growing in clumps where the road surface had cracked, I did not think that this would be a contender for Scotland's busiest road of the year.

The road snaked, dipped and climbed through coarse grassland and rough sedge-coloured moorland, slashed here and there by ancient, dark-chocolate coloured peat hags, and sporadically brightened by purple-pink patches of ling and bell heather.

As the road climbed steeply along the flank of Beinn na Lice, I began to feel a strain and tug at the muscles of my legs, and so I stopped for a breather beside a swift running burn. Wheatears and wagtails flitted and chirped by the water's edge, and the short grass around the grey rock on which I sat, was flecked yellow and white with tormentil and eyebright.

By late afternoon I had reached the green painted, iron gate which led onto Northern Lighthouse Board property, and the private access road to Mull of Kintyre lighthouse. This access road almost defies written description in the abrupt way in which it plummets in a sheer, steep, serpentine drop which eventually comes to a halt at the white-washed lighthouse and accommodation buildings below. When I had called in at Covesea Skerries, Duncan Macpherson, who had been staying there, was an ex-Mull of Kintyre lightkeeper, and he maliciously took a great delight in describing the horror of a road to me. He had not exaggerated.

Before I tackled the descent, I thought back on the history of this place. The Mull of Kintyre was only the second lighthouse to be built by the Northern Lighthouse Board. This was way back in 1788, the year in which people were celebrating the centenary of the 'glorious revolution', and the court doctors had diagnosed George III as insane. King George liked to talk to trees, and if certain newspaper reports about Prince Charles and his plants are to be believed, it would seem to be a trait that has run in the family.

After warily negotiating the steep descent, with one hand constantly on the roadside fence in case my momentum, aided by the weight of my backpack, sent me hurtling in a headlong rush into the dwelling house at the bottom, I finally entered the lighthouse courtyard, thankful to be on the flat once more. As soon as I had arrived I was hailed by a shout, and I turned to see principal lightkeeper Magnus Leask, assistant lightkeeper George Mackay, and local assistant lightkeeper Harry Campbell, sitting on the steps of the lighthouse bothy, watching a pair of yachts tacking about in the Irish sea, far below.

I strolled over to join them, and experienced the 'Jock Tamson's bairn's syndrome' when I discovered that George came from the village of Strathy which is about twenty-five miles from my home in Thurso. We found that we had many friends in common outwith the lighthouse service, and I was pleased to bring him up-to-date with the news from the north. Magnus signed my check-in sheet, and Harry directed me into the first class bothy where I was going to spend the night.

The three Kintyre lightkeepers went off about their various businesses and left me to my own devices. Harry Campbell popped into the bothy after a while and told me that he was going off watch and heading home to his croft. He kindly left me a tin of soup and a couple of rounds of sandwiches, all of which I made short work of a short time later. That night I spent a quiet evening in the bothy watching the movie 'Grand Prix', which was being screened for at least the third time in my memory.

Wakening up fairly early the next morning, I rose, washed and packed, and then sat outside on the bothy steps looking out to sea where I watched a lone lobster fisherman hauling in his creels, and waited for George Mackay to get up. To save me retracing my steps of the past two days, George had agreed to give me a lift in the lighthouse station Land Rover to a point on the west coast of Kintyre which was roughly equidistant with Claonig where I had originally landed. From this point I planned to restart my march northwards.

After an hour or so George duly appeared and I piled into the front seat of the Land Rover. Looking up at the forbidding hill which I had so perilously descended the previous afternoon, I thought to myself that this lift would be well worth it even if it only extended to the end of this particular stretch of road!

The barren moorland flashed by as we headed back along the same stretch of quiet road which I had walked along the day before. Leaving this road we turned off to drive past the busy American air base at Machrihanish, and then northwards past the long, sandy beaches of Kintyre's western seaboard. George finally wished me good luck and farewell at a place called Ballochrey which looked out over the Sound of Gigha to the island of the same modest name. Gigha means 'God's island'.

Showers of light drizzle interrupted occasionally what was otherwise a pleasant and sunny day. The traffic was reasonably light, consisting mainly of tourists with many caravans, caravanettes, tourers and foreign registration plates in evidence.

At the extreme northern end of the Kintyre peninsula, I walked along the shore of West Loch Tarbet. It was here back in the late 9th century where king Magnus Bare-legs of Norway took possession of the entire Kintyre peninsula after a bit of sharp practice involving the terms of a treaty struck up with Edgar, King of Scotland. The treaty granted Magnus sovereignty of all the islands he could sail his longship around. Not being content with just the Hebrides, Magnus had his warriors haul his longship out of the water at West Loch Tarbet and pulled bodily across the narrow isthmus of land to be re-launched in East Loch Tarbet on the other side. All through this operation, the wily Norse king sat in his longship with his hand on the tiller, and thereby acquired sovereignty over the entire Kintyre peninsula. There was not a lot King Edgar of Scotland could do about it at the time, and Kintyre remained in Norse hands until Alexander III of Scotland defeated the Norse forces at the battle of Largs in 1263.

By late afternoon I had arrived at the old centre of the loch Fyne herring industry, the pleasant little town of Tarbert, where I intended staying for the night. I found the town was all abuzz as today was the final day of the local festival week which the good citizens of Tarbert were avidly celebrating. They were receiving a certain amount of assistance in these celebrations from a motley collection of visiting yachtsmen; the crews of what boats still remained of the loch Fyne fishing fleet and the ship's company of the Royal Navy minesweeper *HMS Bossington*. The pubs had been open all day and a good time was obviously being had by all. Always a great believer in the old maxim, 'When in Rome etc.,' I joined in the fun.

The town seemed to be temporarily suspended in a beautiful state of what I can only describe as organized chaos. There appeared to be numerous events, shows and competitions going on at the same time, and as I have already said the pubs were open all day, and all packed out. In one particular hotel, I discovered the cook from the navy ship *Bossington* serving behind the bar, and the ship's electrician was deputizing as waiter, while the equally drunk landlord sat slumped in a corner muttering "Another hour's work should finally clear your bar bills!"

In another pub I fell into conversation with the local coastguard officer, an Irishman with a wicked sense of humour. He introduced me to the manager of the local Clydesdale bank, who also had the surname of Cassells, but was unfortunately not a relation. I have always fancied having a cousin or an uncle who was a bank manager.

The coastguard and myself found that we had much in common. I am an auxiliary coastguard myself when I am on Stroma island, and we also discovered that we had both been in the Communications branch of the Royal Navy. More drink was consumed as we 'swung the lantern'.

Eventually I pitched my bivouac on the shore of East Loch Tarbert. Well, I don't actually remember doing this, but that is where I woke up the next morning.

I came to nursing a splitting headache. On poking this tormented part of my anatomy out of the bivouac door, I was immediately assailed by the age old curse of the west coast of Scotland. Midges! Puffing furiously at a cigarette in an attempt to keep these terrible creatures at bay, I hastily struck down the bivouac and packed my gear away. Shouldering my backpack I beat a hasty retreat through the town, leaving the mist-shrouded lochside with its hordes of miniature man-eaters, as quickly as possible.

While making my way through Tarbert I came upon a marvellous amenity which I wish was more popular with other local councils. A public shower. Fifty pence worth of piping hot water, and a good shampoo and scrub, chased away the hangover and left me feeling brand new.

A light westerly breeze sprang up driving away the early morning mist but bringing a salt-tanged, light drizzle in its place. It was to be a weary, uninteresting and uneventful day's walk through the thickly wooded countryside on the fringe of Knapdale and along the shore of Loch Fyne. There was little to see but the rain dripping tree trunks and branches, thinning out in places for the occasional fleeting glimpse of the grey waters of the loch. Even Radio Scotland chattering away from my backpack transistor radio, seemed more boring than usual that day.

My interest in my surroundings became rejuvenated when I reached Ardrishaig where I stopped to look at the shipping waiting to go through the lock and into the Crinan canal. After half an hour or so of this diversion, I called in at the nearby pub to treat myself to a pint before continuing on my way into neighbouring Lochgilphead where I intended stopping for the night.

Four Irish yachtsmen were in the pub, killing time with nips of whisky and half-pint Guinness chasers, as they waited for their boat's turn to enter the Crinan canal loch. I think all four of them had kissed the Blarney stone at some time or other in the past, because the quick fire comments they fired at each other were hilarious to overhear. One of them asked the barman where was the gents toilet situated. The barman pointed vaguely to the back of the pub and said: "Over there. Just follow your nose." To which one of the other Irishmen immediately replied: "Jesus! You shouldn't have said that to him. He'll be walking around in circles all afternoon!"

The first of the Glasgow Fair holidaymakers had arrived in Lochgilphead and so had the Glasgow Fair weather. As I arrived in the town the drizzle cleared and it really began to rain. I hastily pitched my bivouac on the local campsite, and set off in search of something to eat, as the rain got worse and worse. The west coast monsoon season had started with a vengeance.

After I had eaten, I left the cafe and could plainly see that things had not improved while I had been tucking into my pie, chips and peas. It was absolutely bucketing it down, and the rain was now accompanied by the occasional lightning flash and peal of thunder. So, having a modicum of common sense, I headed for the nearest pub to patiently wait until the situation eased.

Although I do not remember the name of the place, it was a friendly little pub and just the sort of place I would have chosen in which to be stormbound. I soon got chatting to the locals, and they sympathized with me about the weather, unanimously blaming it on the Glasgow Fair

. . . I had become thoroughly convinced that my bivouac must have floated off . . .

holiday. The evening seemed to pass all too quickly, but by closing time the rain was as heavy as ever, and by now I had become thoroughly convinced that my bivouac must have floated off down the loch. A local girl called Maggie Burnett took pity and kindly offered me the use of her spare room for the night. I did not stop to think twice before gratefully accepting.

It was dry the next morning when I pessimistically ventured back to the campsite. Up above me was a pale, watery sun which shone apologetically through thin grey cloud which suggested that the rain would not be long in returning. Past a row of caravans I saw the reassuring sight of a low-lying, orange blob which was undoubtedly my bivouac. It had not sailed off down Loch Fyne after all. Approaching the bivvy I found that things were bad enough anyway. Just about all of my gear, sleeping bag etc. was soaking wet. A huge pool of water had formed in a dip in the bivouac roof, which the local midges were using as a swimming pool. I dried out what I could with my towel which had been in my backpack and was reasonably dry. Then I finished mopping up the interior of the bivouac with the pages of that morning's newspaper which I had bought from a nearby newsagent, and had not even read yet. This mopping up with the paper so impressed me with its effectiveness that ever after I made it a practice to buy a newspaper whenever I could. When I camped for the night, I would spread the sheets of the newspaper over the inside of the groundsheet, and in this way it was excellent for soaking up any small leaks should it rain during the night, or easing the volume of water which was to eventually begin coming through the larger leaks.

Once I had packed my soggy gear, I headed off out of Lochgilphead and into the scenic Argyll countryside. A short distance from the town and I happened to glance to my left. What I saw had me wondering if I had taken too much drink the previous evening. I stood and stared at what I could plainly see was a ship's masthead slowly moving above the tops of the trees lining the road. Just before I was about to swear off the demon drink forever, I remembered the Crinan canal, and sure enough, on looking at my map I saw that at this point it ran parallel to the road.

This part of the country which I was now walking through, was once the ancient kingdom of Dalriada where the Scots from Ireland first settled back in the days of such heroes as Niall of the nine hostages and Conn of a hundred battles. I walked past the green, rock-studded remains of the hill fort of Dunadd which archaeologists and historians believe was the capital of the early Scots kings of Dalriada. From this small foothold here far in the west, over the course of the next few hundred years, the Scots were to steadily displace and overrun the long established Picts, giving our nation the name we know it by today, 'Scotland'.

I stopped briefly at the village of Kilmartin. As my earlier prediction of rain had not proved itself, but on the contrary, a hot, yellow sun was shining out of a clear blue sky, I decided to eat my lunch al fresco. Sitting on my backpack alongside the wall surrounding the old graveyard of Kilmartin, I tucked into bread and cold meat while I watched a busload of daytrippers, cameras at the ready, dutifully follow a guide into the graveyard to view the famous Kilmartin sculptured stones.

Indeed this area seemed to be steeped in stonework of antiquity, and I passed several cairns and groups of standing stones as I walked up the A816, hoping to arrive at Arduaine by nightfall.

It would seem to be a day for me getting my predictions and estimates all wrong, because I arrived at Arduaine far earlier than I had anticipated. It was one of those days in which I felt full of walking, the weather was good, the roads were fairly level, and the traffic was fairly light, and so I just pushed on. I finally stopped in the cool of the late evening and put up my bivouac for the night at Kininver. I decided that I must have completed a good day's walk of at least thirty miles. Tired, but very satisfied with the day's progress, and delighted that the threatened rain had never materialized, I crawled inside of my erected bivouac. No sooner had I zipped up the door and crawled into my still damp sleeping bag, when I heard the familiar pitter patter on the nylon roof. I was too dog-tired to care, if the bivvy leaked there was little I could do about it now, so I casually slipped off to sleep.

The bivvy did leak. A combination of a sopping wet sleeping bag and a steady drip of water on my head, woke me up early the next morning. Not exactly feeling full of the joys of spring, I crouched into the driest corner of the bivouac and breakfasted on a bottle of lucozade and a couple of slices of bread, the remains of my lunch in the sunshine at Kilmartin.

I glanced at my watch and noticed that the time was only five thirty. This would be my earliest start yet, as I saw little point in trying to go back to sleep. On consulting my map, I saw that I was only a matter of eight or nine miles from the town of Oban, so after dismantling and packing the bivouac, I set off hoping to arrive in Oban early enough to have a complete day in hand to dry and clean my clothes and gear. There was also a Northern Lighthouse Board stores depot situated in the town and I had planned to call there.

The rain eased and then abruptly ceased completely just as I arrived in Oban. Threading my way through the town, I made for the seafront to where I knew the lighthouse depot was situated, just along the shore from the railway station and the ferry depot. The place was just opening for the day's work when I arrived. I was made welcome by storeman Sandy Pirie, and from his office I 'phoned up headquarters to advise them of my whereabouts as they had not heard from me since Corsewall lighthouse. I had arrived at the Mull of Kintyre lighthouse on a Saturday night when the head office was closed for the weekend.

Sandy told me that he was expecting the lighthouse tender the MV *Fingal*, to berth in Oban later that day. This seemed to me good news, as I thought that I might be able to get a bed aboard the ship rather than find somewhere to spend the night in Oban, or bivouac on the town's outskirts. But first I had some essential business to attend to. Leaving my backpack and bivouac in the safekeeping of the lighthouse store, I filled two carrier bags with dirty, wet clothing and headed for the nearest laundromat.

While my dirty laundry happily churned round and round in the laundromat washing machine, I went for a wander around Oban. The following day I was planning to indulge in another bit of island hopping, by catching the ferry to the island of Mull, and then taking another ferry from Tobermorey on Mull to Mingary on the Ardnamurchan peninsula. I had to call in at the lighthouse at Ardnamurchan Point, and by taking this overseas route I would save approximately five days of walking - the time it would have taken me if I had stuck to the mainland and followed the circuitous route via the Corran Ferry.

As I idled about the harbour, I spotted the Caledonian MacBrayne booking office and decided on impulse to call in and see if they would allow me a free passage on their ferries. A pretty girl at the ticket desk directed me to the office of the area manager, a Mr. Horne. When I explained to him about my walk, he was more than helpful and immediately provided me with free tickets for the next morning's ferries. He also gave me his card and office 'phone number should I require any more assistance from Cal-Mac during my journey.

I returned to the laundromat to collect my clothes. Looking up I could see the peculiar structure known as McCaig's Tower, glowering down on the town. McCaig was a banker and art critic. He had the tower built between 1890 and 1900 as a sort of philanthropic, early jobs-creation scheme, providing employment for locally unemployed masons. The town was thronged with tourists and holidaymakers eagerly buying cheap and not so cheap souvenirs, principally of the 'tartan tat' variety. Still everyone seemed happy enough, particularly the Oban shopkeepers.

As I returned to collect my backpack from the lighthouse store, I took a long detour the length of the sea front, and spotted the lighthouse tender *Fingal* nosing her way into the harbour. I slowly strolled along to her customary berth alongside the lighthouse depot, pacing myself to arrive there just as the ship came alongside.

At the time of writing, the Northern Lighthouse Board maintains three lighthouse tenders, though the future of these fine ships, and indeed the service in general, is still under review. The ships are as follows: the MV *Fingal* which is based in Oban and principally used for work around the Isle of Man, the Hebrides, and the west coast of Scotland; *MV Pole Star* is based in Stromness, Orkney, and carries out most of its work around Orkney, Shetland, and the lighthouses situated on the north coast of Scotland; and finally the flagship of this small fleet, the *MV Pharos* which deals with the Firth of Forth and east coast, and carries the Commissioners of the Northern Lighthouse Board on their annual tour of inspection around a selected number of lighthouses each summer.

The lighthouse tenders are used for a wide variety of jobs such as delivering bulky spare parts, stores and supplies, and fuel to offshore lighthouses, checking and maintaining navigational buoys and unmanned lighthouses. Until comparatively recent times when the use of chartered helicopters has largely taken over the job, the tenders were responsible for the relief change-over of lightkeepers at offshore lighthouses. All three of the fleet are handsome looking ships. With their black hulls, spotless wooden decks, gleaming white superstructure and buff funnels, each and every one is kept as immaculate as any flagship of a Royal Navy battle fleet.

I boarded the *Fingal* and was taken to see Captain Forth the master. He heard out my request and readily consented to my staying the night on board. One of the ship's stewards directed me to the now largely unused lightkeepers' accommodation cabins where I settled myself in. On having a quick look around, I discovered the crew's drying room on the next deck up from my cabin, and I took the opportunity of spreading my sleeping bag and bivouac out on the wooden trellis above the hot pipes, to air and dry them.

That night I wandered into Oban for something to eat and to be ripped off over the price of a pint of beer in a certain hotel bar. I was not looking for a night on the town, so I returned back on board the *Fingal* fairly early. I checked my gear in the drying room, and on finding that my bivouac was dry, I lugged it back down to my cabin and subjected it to a good all over spraying with an aerosol of silicone waterproofing. Although it was a little after eight in the evening, the previous day's long walk, followed by a night of little sleep, began to catch up with me. After packing the bivvy into its holding bag, I crawled into the bunk provided for me and dozed off to sleep the sleep of the dead.

I felt slightly disorientated when I first awoke the next morning. Feeling the gentle bobbing motion of the ship, hearing the whine of generators, smelling the sharp stink of diesel, and seeing the morning light come streaming through a ship-side scuttle, I believed for one confused moment that I was back at sea in the Royal Navy. But my wits soon gathered themselves and were positively consolidated over a breakfast of mugs of strong, hot tea sweetened with two large spoonfuls of sugar and brewed by one of the *Fingal's* seamen who had been left on board to act as ship watchkeeper. Finishing my second cup, I went to the drying room and was pleased to find that my sleeping bag had completely dried out during the night. Packing the sleeping bag away and shouldering my backpack, I disembarked from the Fingal and crossed over to the adjacent quayside where I joined the first of the passengers embarking on board the Caledonian-MacBrayne ferry MV *Caledonia*.

There was still a good half hour or so before the ferry was due to leave, and I settled myself into a comfortable seat in the saloon to await our departure for the short crossing of the Firth of Lorn. Very soon the ferry was bustling with tourists and backpackers of almost every description and some who defied description. Then with a slight lurch, and a change of engine note, we were off.

Three teenage French girls took up the seats directly opposite to me. One of these girls, a dark-haired, dark-eyed, petite Gallic beauty about seventeen years old, passed the time and the journey by quite outrageously flirting with yours truly. I hope that young mademoiselle realized that she made a happy man feel very old.

With a slight jarring bump the ferry nudged the wooden pilings of the jetty at Craignure on the island of Mull. Here I disembarked and boarded the bus which would take me through to the island's principal town of Tobermory, a quaint sounding name which is derived from the Gaelic 'Tobar Mhoire', which when translated into English simply means 'Mary's Well'.

A steady shower of rain pattered against the dirt-encrusted windows of the bus, obscuring and greying the Mull countryside. I took a seat at the back of the bus, a good distance away from French female teenagers, and read a paper which I had bought the previous day but had never got around to reading. It is quite a common trait among lightkeepers to read old newspapers. When you are serving your tour of duty out at a remote lighthouse, there is obviously no daily delivery of papers. I have seen some lightkeepers quite delightedly reading a three week old copy of a Sunday newspaper they had found being used as wrapping for groceries which had been sent out from the shore.

The bus pulled into Tobermory, a town I had last visited when I was a schoolboy of twelve or thirteen. I had been at a sea-scout camp at nearby Dunstaffanage castle, from where we had gone on an expedition to Mull. My initial impression of the place that day as I alighted from the bus, was that the town had changed very little over the intervening years. I strolled along the seafront and noted that there was the usual handful of visiting yachts anchored in the bay and I watched a small inflatable cruise past, manned by four characters dressed in scuba diving gear. I thought, no doubt another bunch of hopefuls looking for the 'Tobermory treasure'.

The tale of the Tobermory treasure is worth recounting here if only to express the moral that it is wise to pay bills promptly to Mull shopkeepers. After the debacle of the Spanish Armada in 1588, the galleon *Almirante De Florencia* had been driven right around the northern tip of Scotland and was beating her way back down the west coast, heading home for Spain. The ship anchored in Tobermory bay to take on provisions and fresh water. After they had taken on their supplies, the Spaniards were confronted by a local man called Donald Maclean, who not unreasonably demanded payment for the goods he had provided them with. The haughty Dons merely locked Maclean up on board their ship, having no intention of paying the bill. Somehow or other, Maclean managed to escape, and to display his displeasure at the Spanish treatment, he broke into the ship's magazine and blew it up, sending the *Almirante De Florencia*, numerous Spaniards, and a rumoured treasure of 30 million ducats, to the sandy bottom of the bay.

Although there have been numerous attempts over the course of the past four hundred years to salvage the Tobermory treasure, apart from a handful of coins, little of real value has been found. Or if there has, whoever found it has kept remarkably quiet about the matter.

I had some time to wait until the sailing of the Mingary ferry, so I sauntered about the seafront, enjoying the sights. There was a cool, west wind blowing which was gradually increasing in strength. When this stiff breeze became accompanied by a heavy shower of rain, I was forced to seek shelter and comfort in the nearby Macdonald Arms. In here I enjoyed a pint or two of beer, and the company of the pretty, red-haired barmaid who told me that she came from the town of Dingwall in Ross-shire, and that she was a niece of Colin Campbell, who is a very funny and very popular comedian in the north of Scotland.

Although the sky was still grey, the rain had eased off when the time came for me to leave the pub and catch the ferry. However, the wind had moved round a couple of points and was blowing cold and strong from the north west. The small ferry bobbed up and down in the slight swell being generated by this breeze. I embarked over the swaying gangway, and being a seasoned small ferry traveller after my years spent in the north isles of Shetland, I wisely disdained the scenery and joined the purser in the small saloon. Here we sat grinning evilly at each other as we listened to the indignant howls and screams of the less knowledgeable, sightseeing tourists as they took an unexpected soaking off the lumps of spray cast over the blunt bows of the ferry by the stiff north westerly wind.

Once the ferry had berthed at Mingary, I bid the purser farewell and walked up past the castle. It had been garrisoned by government troops sent to hunt out rebel Jacobite sympathisers in the area, during the bloody days of suppression immediately after Culloden.

Heading through the sprawling village of Kilchoan, I took the single track road which would lead me to the most westerly part of the Scottish mainland, Ardnamurchan, 'the point of the sea-dogs'.

I walked through a wild and rugged countryside, my passage watched warily by black-faced sheep as they grazed on the rough grasses between the gorse bushes and clumps of bracken. One or two cars passed me by, but there was little sign of other human beings except for the small farms, crofts and holiday homes dotted sporadically about the place. Finally, I rounded a corner and followed the road onto the rocky promontory where I could plainly see the light-tower sticking up into the air like a long, granite needle.

Ardnamurchan Point lighthouse was built in 1894, and from this lonely corner of Scotland looks out across the water to the island of Coll in the south and Rhum, Eigg, and Muck to the north. The light-tower itself has the distinctive and I think unique feature of not being painted the customary eye-dazzling white, but has been left in the naturally unadorned state of dressed granite. As I approached the place, the afternoon sun broke out through the clouds for a brief minute or two, and shone on the tower causing the small flecks of mica in the granite to shimmer and sparkle like thousands of tiny diamond chips.

On my arrival I spoke briefly to principal lightkeeper Jim Hardie, who in a couple of weeks would be entertaining a slightly better known visitor to his lighthouse. This was none other than Her Majesty the Queen, who was to visit Ardnamurchan to commemorate the Northern Lighthouse Board Bicentenary. Jim duly signed my check-in sheet and apologized that he could not hang around for long as he was off to his bed in preparation for an early start the next day when he was off on leave. He no doubt had quite a lot on his mind at the time as well.

The lighthouse bothy was to be my shelter for the night. I knew this place of old, having been stationed here briefly when I was a supernumary

Ardnamurchan lighthouse
courtesy of Christopher Nicholson

lightkeeper. Ian, the local assistant lightkeeper, was on duty that night so I shared the bothy with him. I remembered him from my last visit to Ardnamurchan, and he was good company. I inherited a book from him before I left, *The Once and Future King* by T.H. White. I had read this book years ago, but thought it well worth reading again. If I should ever be asked to recommend a book to read of a night in a soggy bivouac, this particular one would be high on the list.

After a good night's sleep, followed by half of the assistant lightkeeper's breakfast, I was given a lift into Kilchoan, from where I began the next stretch of my walk.

Most of that daywas spent traversing the Ardnamurchan peninsula, walking the length of the only road which leads in and out of Ardnamurchan. Geologists have stated that the entire Ardnamurchan peninsula was once an enormous volcano. The hillocks, crags and rocky outcrops which have been left after millenia of weathering, is both impressive and wildly beautiful. In an almost treeless landscape, outcrops of grey-black volcanic rock sprout through the short sage-green grass, and the darker green patches of bracken. Through this rugged landscape the road curved around the flank of Beinn Hiant, which in English means 'Holy mountain', which set in such barren scenery did not need too much of a stretch of the imagination to picture some ancient, Celtic Moses ascending to the summit of this mountain in the wilderness, to commune with God. A couple of miles further on, the scenery was softened by the occasional copse of trees as the road began to descend and run parallel with the shore of Loch Sunart. Yachts and pleasure craft skimmed to and fro upon the still, green-black waters, and here and there, thigh-booted anglers hopefully cast from the shore.

I lingered for a while at the top of the afternoon, in thickly wooded Glenborrodale. I had bought some provisions at the general store in Kilchoan, and sitting on my backpack I listened to a programme about hill shepherds in the borders, on Radio Scotland, and feasted on a light lunch of cold meat sandwiches followed by a couple of apples for dessert. Directly opposite, across the road from me, an ancient birch tree sprouted razor strop fungus which put me in mind of an impudent schoolboy poking his tongue out. Red dead nettles, thistles, dandelions, and yes, you have guessed it, foxgloves, grew in abundance on the verge where I was sitting.

Around tea time that day I arrived at the village of Salen, which had been my provisional choice of somewhere to camp for the evening. I first decided to stop for a pint in the local hostelry. Here I sat in a quiet corner and enjoyed my drink while I watched a party of tourists who seemed to have enjoyed a good many drinks, providing the entertainment.

The weather had been pretty good all day. Not oppressively hot, but dry with a cool breeze and a high, full cover of cloud. Looking away from the antics of the drunken tourists, I glanced through the pub window and came to an immediate decision that as the weather seemed to be holding fair, I would make the most of it and push on a little further before camping for the night.

As it turned out, I did not walk all that much further but came to a halt three miles past Salen at the village of Acharacle, at the head of Loch Shiel. The shores of this loch were once the site of the ancient mustering place of the warriors of the once mighty clan Ranald. They would gather here when the clan was preparing to go to war. Reports say that over 300 of them gathered here in 1745 when the clan came out for the Pretender.

After I had first inquired of one of the locals, I was told that the shore of the loch was common land, and it would be quite all right for me to pitch my bivouac anywhere I chose in that area. I followed a rutted track down to the lochside where I chose a dry, reasonably level patch of ground near a ramshackle boatshed. Here I began to set up camp despite the deprivations of the local midges which soon got to know of my whereabouts.

Once I had the bivouac erected to my satisfaction, and my gear stowed safely within, I headed for the local hotel which was only about eight hundred yards away. The neat little public bar was full of anglers swapping lies about their day's fishing out on the loch. Over a pint of beer I chatted for a while with the landlady and her son. The son asked me if I spoke Gaelic, to which I replied that I knew a little, but it was not, nor ever had been a language spoken greatly in Caithness. On hearing this reply, his mother was quick to comment: "Ach yes. They all speak bloody Norse up there!"

While I was in the bar I discovered that there was to be a dance held later that night in the village hall. With a great effort of will I declined the suggestions that I should attend, excusing myself on the grounds of being too tired after a long day's walking. But to tell the truth, the reason I did not go was because I have attended many west coast country dances over the years, and I fully intended pushing on the next day, and not in two or three days time which may well have been the case had I weakened and gone along to the local hop.

... *"Ach yes. They all speak bloody Norse up there!"* ...

That night there was a light but continuous rain and despite my earlier attempts at water-proofing, the bivouac leaked like a sieve. This was a state of affairs with which I was to become well accustomed over the course of the final couple of weeks.

Sheets of drizzle streamed in waves across Loch Shiel in the grey light of morning as I dismantled and packed the bivouac. The wetness made life a bit uncomfortable but at least it succeeded in grounding the local midge population. With my gear packed and secured I headed off to re-join the main road and make a desperate, early morning search for a public toilet. This search proved unfruitful, but being ever practical, I wandered into the nearest patch of dense woodland and emulated the wild bear.

. . . and emulated the wild bear . . .

The drizzle progressed into full-blooded rain, and an unseasonably cold wind began to blow. A mistaken turning leading me to walk over a mile out of my way, did little to help matters. I passed a pale white, roadside statue of the Virgin Mary outside a Roman Catholic chapel near Dalnabreck. I stopped and stared at the statue for a few minutes, but no miracles. It wasn't tears running down the Madonna's stone cheeks, but trickling rain drops.

The road began to climb steeply as I rounded Loch Moidart and turned directly into the teeth of the bitter wind and driving rain. I could see below me, surrounded by the grey, foam-flecked waters of the loch, the miserable and abandoned ruins of Castle Tioram. Once a mighty stronghold and the home of the chiefs of Clan Ranald for over four hundred years, and now just a jumble of stonework at the water's edge.

Cold, wet, miserable, I trudged over the summit of Glenuig hill. The landscape presented a drab picture of water running over the grey rocks and dripping, sodden bracken. Even the hardy, black-faced hill sheep looked totally dejected.

On the other side of the hill at the inlet of Glenuig Bay, I saw a welcome sight — the Glenuig Hotel. I made an immediate bee-line for it with a fresh spring in my step. Despite it being well on in the summer season, there was a blazing log fire in the grate of the hotel bar. As I revived myself with a pint of foaming beer and a large rum, I sat so close to this fire that my clothes began to steam. I could have quite willingly sat there all day but I had to push on to Lochailort where I intended camping for the night. With a sigh of resignation, I handed my empty glass to the barmaid, hauled on my waterproofs and made my way outside to once more face the elements.

The remainder of that day's walk was far from enjoyable, just a progression of one step after another as I forged through the wind and rain. I took little notice of my surroundings and my brain switched on to automatic pilot. I gratefully arrived at Lochailort by late afternoon, but here I had some news which caused me to drastically change my plans. My original intention had been to find somewhere to camp in the region of Lochailort that night, and in the morning push on to Mallaig where I intended catching the ferry across to Armadale on the Isle of Skye. However, purely on the off-chance I overheard in the Lochailort pub that because the following day was a Sunday there would be no ferry service between Mallaig and Armadale until the Monday morning. On making further inquiries I was told that there was one last ferry still to run that evening. This one sailed from Mallaig at seven thirty. In ten minutes time there would be a train due in Lochailort station which connected with this ferry.

Suffering a minor crisis of conscience, I debated the ethics of catching this train. A two day stopover in this region and in this weather, did not appeal to me in the slightest, and I argued to myself that with ferry trips and island hopping, what I was doing was far different from a conventional sponsored walk anyway. What the hell, I thought, it was not as if I was out to claim any kind of record or seeking fame and glory for some athletic feat of endurance, I was out to enjoy myself as much as possible. As matters stood, I had already walked a good deal further than John O'Groats to Lands End, and I still had about 300 miles to go.

My mind made up, I headed to Lochailort station to catch the train, the persistence of the rain persuading me of the wisdom of my decision. I discovered a fellow backpacker already waiting at the station. This chap was organized, he had huddled himself into a corner of the perspex-sided shelter on the station platform, and in here he was tending a steaming pan of soup which he was cooking on a hissing primus stove.

I had not long to wait for the train, which with me aboard was soon rattling along the solitary track which snakes through the Arisaig countryside to the bustling little west coast fishing port of Mallaig.

Looking through the carriage window I could see the wind whipping up flecks of white on the dark grey waters of Loch Nan Uamh, 'the loch of the cave'. This remote sea loch was the scene of a minor sea battle on April 29th 1746, when the Royal Navy ships *Greyhound* and *Terror* surprised the French frigates *Bellona* and *Mars*, shortly after the Frenchmen had landed stores, arms, and money to aid the already doomed Jacobite cause. Legend has it that some of the Jacobite gold is still buried somewhere on the loch shore.

Not long after this skirmish, the loch was again visited by two French ships, *L'Heureux* and the *Prince de Conti*. This time the reason behind the clandestine visit was to spirit away into an ignominious exile the Young Pretender, Prince Charles Edward Stuart.

It was only a very short journey, and very soon the train was pulling into Mallaig station. Shouldering my backpack I alighted and headed off for the short walk to the harbour and the ferry for Skye. The harbour was packed with fishing boats, their white registration markings representing nearly every major fishing port in Scotland. Casting a casual eye over them, I could see the BCK of Buckie; FR of Fraserburgh; PD of Peterhead; and just to remind me of home I spotted two boats bearing the WK registration of Wick. A rank smell of rotted fish and stale diesel fumes hung over the harbour, while gulls clamoured and screeched among the wooden fish boxes littering the quayside.

It seemed no sooner had I boarded the ferry than we were casting off. During the bumpy crossing of the Sound of Sleat, I struck up a conversation with three Australians who told me that they were doing a long, slow tour of Britain, relying on finding casual work here and there to keep them in funds. As the ferry came into dock at Armadale, the Aussies told me that they intended driving up to Portree that night, and did I fancy a lift? This offer gave me pause for thought. My original plan had been to find somewhere near Armadale to erect the bivvy for the night, and then in the morning push on to Kyleakin and catch the ferry there to Kyle of Lochalsh back on the mainland. I had been assured that this ferry did run on Sundays. But, by catching the train at Lochairlort, and then the Mallaig ferry, I was now a full day ahead of schedule. I had some good friends in Portree with whom I knew that I would be more than welcome to stay should I turn up unexpectedly. So I promptly made the decision that it was time for a day off, and I accepted the Aussies' offer of a lift.

The Aussies' car, a Ministry of Transport inspector's nightmare, in the shape of an ageing Cortina of several different colours but principally the reddish brown of rust, rattled into Portree at about nine thirty that evening. In the town square we parted company, as they set off to find somewhere to stay for the night, and I headed for the bar of the Portree Hotel from where I 'phoned my friends Tommy and Thelma Budge, the parents of Sandra, who I had met in Edinburgh. In a matter of fifteen minutes, the pair of them were in the pub with me and we were having a reunion.

Portree is a pleasant little town. The place was originally called Kiltragleann, but was renamed Port Righ, which is the Gaelic for 'Port of the King', in honour of a royal visit to the island of Skye by James V of Scotland. It was here that Charles Edward Stuart — one time pretender to the British throne, and patron saint of tartan tat souvenir vendors, and second rate folk singers — said farewell to Flora Macdonald, the lady who provided him with the clothes for his historically famous drag act as the maid Bessie Burke.

That night I sat up quite late with Tommy and Thelma as we caught up with each other's news. Finally I went off to revel in the luxury of sleeping in a warm, dry, bed instead of a damp, soggy bivouac. The familiar sound of raindrops bouncing off the bedroom window only served to make the experience all the more enjoyable. Upon rising in the late morning, I tackled Thelma's washing machine and tumble drier, laundering my clothes and thoroughly drying out my sleeping bag which had taken a soaking during my overnight stop at Acharacle. The rest of that day I regarded literally as 'lazy Sunday' and did as little as possible but rest up, drink Tommy's whisky and watch the telly.

Monday morning dawned and time for me to restart my walk. The bus which would take me to the ferry at Kyleakin, was not due to leave Portree until one o'clock in the afternoon, and so I took the opportunity to do some shopping. I called in at a busy little general store where I stocked up on iron rations of tinned corned beef and 'Stockans' thin oatcakes. Although I had not normally bothered to carry goods around with me as I had quite successfully relied on the likes of bar lunches and the odd shop or cafe which I might encounter on the day's hike, I thought it prudent to start carrying provisions with me now as I realized that it would not always be so easy to find somewhere where I might get a meal in the sparsely populated north western portion of my walk.

Sometime during the course of the past couple of weeks I had managed to lose two of the aluminium ferrules which joined together the thin poles which supported the canopy of my bivouac. The last couple of times I had camped, I had improvised by taping the poles together with insulation tape, but this was far from satisfactory and the poles tended to sag and did little to improve the already sadly deficient waterproof qualities of the bivvy. Whilst I was in Portree with a bit of time on my hands, I hit upon the bright idea of calling in at a plumber's shop and obtaining a couple of short lengths of copper pipe of a fractionally larger diameter than the bivouac support poles. When I explained to the plumber just what I wanted such small pieces of pipe for, he was so tickled with the idea that he willingly gave me the pieces for nothing, and I am pleased to say that when I tried them out, they worked a treat. Mind you, the bloody bivouac still leaked!

Returning to Tommy and Thelma's house to pick up my gear, I decided to take the opportunity to 'phone Rubh Re lighthouse, the next lighthouse I was to visit. It was a good job that I took the bother to 'phone, as the lightkeeper who answered the 'phone informed me that he and his fellow keepers were just waiting for a car to come and pick them up. This was the last day that Rubh Re would be a manned lighthouse, from that afternoon the place would be fully automatic. Another one gone, I thought sadly to myself as I bade the Budges farewell and headed off to catch the bus.

For some reason which I never discovered, I had a long wait for the Kyleakin bus, and it was a full two hours late in leaving Portree. As we speeded through the picturesque Skye countryside, heading for the ferry, I decided that it would not be worth walking very far that day, but that I would bivouac for the night somewhere in the region of Kyle of Lochalsh.

There was a campsite marked on my map which I estimated to be about six miles inland from Kyle of Lochalsh, and it was here I intended stopping for the night. Alighting from the ferry I started to walk up the steep hill which leads out of the town, but my heart was far from in it. About a mile out of the town I gave up and pitched my bivouac on a level patch of rough, waste ground adjacent to a lay-by, and overlooking the swift running waters of Kyle Akin where King Hakon of Norway had once moored his longships on their way to defeat at the hands of the Scots army at the battle of Largs in 1263. Looking down from my campsite, I could see military shipping still moored there, though of course not now the dragon-prowed longships of the Norsemen, but a small flotilla of modern Royal Navy MFVs. and fleet tenders.

It was too early in the evening to settle down for the night in the bivouac, so retracing my steps I walked back down the hill into Kyle of Lochalsh with the intention of sampling a pint or two of the local beer before I turned in for the night. Descending the brae, I watched the Skye ferry passing back and forth on the short crossing between the island and the mainland, and I wondered to myself just how long it would be before a bridge spanned the narrow channel. The sun, now low and watery in the west, shone on the ruins of castle Noil, an ancient stronghold of the Mackinnon clan, and possibly one of the most photographed ruins on the west coast.

I did not linger long in Kyle of Lochalsh as I found the two pubs which I visited unbearably quiet and depressing. Under threatening clouds, just discernible in the twilight, I shuffled back to my bivouac and bed.

It poured with rain again that night, completely undoing my work of drying out my sleeping bag, as despite the strengthened support poles and yet another generous application of waterproof sealant, the damn bivvy still leaked. After having spent a fairly inactive day the day before, I found myself awake in the early morning, crouched with my soggy sleeping bag in the one dry corner of the bivvy, as I feasted on oatcakes, corned beef, and a slightly wormy apple. To pass the time I alternately read the *Once and Future King*, or watched drops of water sporadically drip from the bivvy roof. During a lull in the downpour, I hastily packed and headed off into the grey morning, leaving the island of Skye and the town of Kyle of Lochalsh behind me, completely shrouded in a drizzle filled mist.

The road ran parallel with the shore of Loch Alsh, the dark waters of the sea loch looking cold and inhospitable in the diffuse grey light of the morning. Across on the other side of the road, pools of standing water in rain sodden fields were evidence enough that the west coast had suffered its usual summer while I had been roasting in the hot sun on the east coast. A friend of mine who lived around these parts for a couple of years, was once bemoaning the west coast weather to me: "It seems to be always bloody well raining!" he moaned. "And when the rain stops for more than an hour, the locals start muttering about the drought!"

I would not deny that the west coast seems to have more than its fair share of rain, but when the weather is fine and sunny, the sheer beauty and grandeur of the scenery makes the occasional soaking a very small price to pay. They say that there is some kind of snake in every paradise.

After walking a couple of miles along the shore of the loch, I left what was the main road to Inverness, to take a secondary route which would cut across country to Loch Carron side. This road climbed steeply past bare tracts of moorland and small pine forests. At the summit of the climb I stopped for a rest and a smoke at the Hydro Electric Board reservoir at Loch Anna. The day was improving with the rain showers becoming less frequent and a pale, ghost of a sun occasionally peeking out from behind the grey, scudding clouds.

At Strome Ferry I left the road which I had been following to detour down to the small village and hotel by the lochside for a couple of lunch-time pints and something to eat. Apart from a couple of forestry workers the large, roomy pub was empty. The forestry men told me that the village was almost a ghost town nowadays, since the ferry had stopped running across Loch Carron.

I spent that afternoon walking along the shore of Loch Carron, the road running parallel with the loch shore and the single track railway line which links the Kyle of Lochalsh with Inverness. Periodically, along with the Inverness-Thurso and Wick line, British Railways bring up the threat of line closure, but thankfully this has not happened yet. I did hear that the train to Kyle of Lochalsh is proving more and more popular with tourists due to the scenic countryside through which it passes.

Tourist traffic passed sporadically, and the occasional heavy, trades vehicle, but on the whole it was a quiet and pleasant road to walk along. Across on the opposite shore of the loch I could plainly see the neat, white painted houses of the village of Lochcarron.

I finally arrived at Strath Carron at the head of the loch, and decided that this was as good a place as any to camp for the night. After a quick look around I pitched my bivouac on a wide swathe of grassy, waste ground by the side of the railway track.

Exactly five hundred years ago in 1486, Strath Carron was the site of a bloody clan battle between the Rosses and the Mackays. Clan Ross came off the worse leaving dead in the quiet strath at the head of the loch, one of the clan chiefs, seventeen officers, and 'a great many common men'. I hoped that the ghosts of these dead clansmen would not return to celebrate their five hundredth anniversary and keep me awake that night, but just in case, I headed for the bar of the Strathcarron Hotel for an encounter with a more agreeable kind of spirit.

I had been sat in the pub for about ten minutes or so, when the front door was pushed open and a half-grown, black and tan mongrel pup entered and swiftly disappeared behind the bar and into the interior of the hotel. A few seconds later the dog was followed by an irate and flustered tourist who loudly inquired in an aggrieved home counties accent, if anyone here in the bar owned a small black and brown dog - a description which perfectly fitted the mongrel pup. The tourist went on to indignantly state that the dog had torn his wife's dress when she had tried to stroke the animal, and that it had actually snarled at him with bared teeth when he had remonstrated with it.

The half dozen or so locals in the bar tutted and shook their heads in sympathy. One old worthy replied that the dog in question sounded like an animal that belonged to a man who lived in the village, 'and just a complete idiot with dogs'. With an angry snort, the tourist turned on his heel and left the pub. Shortly later we could hear his car revving up as he drove off. At this point, the local who had volunteered the information about the dog to the disgruntled tourist, turned to the landlord, who had kept very quiet throughout, and said in frank admiration: "Man, John. That is a fine wee doggie you have, right enough. That is the third Englishman he has gone for this month!"

Later that evening the rains came down again, and although it was another sopping wet night in the bivouac, I slept soundly enough despite the dampness. With the coming of daylight, the rain had eased to a light drizzle which had itself completely cleared away by the time I decided to rise and get going.

I breakfasted on oatcakes washed down with lucozade, after which I attempted to dry out as much of the bivouac's interior as possible with a three day old 'Daily Record' newspaper. After I had mopped up as much of the loose water as possible, I crawled out into the light of day and saw that the bright orange roof of the bivouac was absolutely crawling with large, black slugs. I do not think that I have ever seen so many of these creatures in the same place at the same time. I wondered if they had been attracted by the bright orange colour, or perhaps the smell of the waterproof sealant which did not work? However, I had not got the time to play at the philosophizing naturalist, so I simply swatted them off with the back of my hand and packed away the bivouac.

Hoisting my backpack onto my shoulders I prepared to set off on the day's hike. At that very moment I spotted the early morning Inverness-bound train approaching the nearby Strathcarron station. It had been my original intention that day to follow the main road to Shieldaig on the

... a fine wee doggie ... that is the third Englishman he has gone for this month! ...

southern shore of Loch Torridon, and there camp overnight. I had debated an alternative route to this which I had noticed when scanning my map in the pub the previous evening. I had seen that there was a forestry road, or rather track, which led across the hills from the next railway station at Achnashellach, to a point on the main road a mile or so from Kinlochewe. I had worked out that this alternative route would cut up to two days off my journey. I instantly made the decision to head for Achnashellach on the arriving train, the decision compounded by the familiar early morning cramps in my stomach which persuaded me of the sense in making use of one of the side benefits of the five minute train journey in a countryside almost completely devoid of public toilets.

Disembarking at the picturesque, sleepy little station of Achnashellach, I was joined on the station platform by three elderly Englishmen. This trio of originals were all suitably attired in sensible brown boots; tweed plus-fours, (or shite-catchers, as this mode of garment is irreverently called in Caithness), thick, woolly jumpers, tweed deerstalker hats and anoraks in Barbour jacket green. Each man clutched a stout, knobbly, walking stick. I was dressed in my well-battered hiking boots, greyish-white sea-boot stockings, track suit trousers — with yellow 'go faster' stripes down each leg, and this entire ensemble was topped off by a RNLI T-shirt with an ever-expanding hole about the vicinity of my navel.

Standing on the lonely platform as the train shuttled off eastwards, we must have made a strange tableau as we regarded each other with equal wariness.

. . . we regarded each other with equal wariness . . .

Upon discovering that I did not bite and was going the same way, the three old gents thawed a little, and walked in company with me to the start of the steeply climbing forestry track. At this point they stopped for a rest and told me to carry on as they would not be able to keep pace with me. "You will probably take off up that hill like a young stag!" one of them chortled.

Not wishing to disappoint them I shot up the sloping pathway with all the speed of a Cumbrian fell runner who knew that there was a pub the other side of the hill. However, they may have been a bit disillusioned to have seen that the 'young stag' stopped and sat down on a tree trunk for a smoke and a five minute rest as soon as he had rounded the first bend and was out of sight.

Proceeding at a more leisurely pace I set off once more. Steadily climbing all the time, the track took me through thickly planted coniferous woodland. My feet trudged through a dense carpet of pine needles, occasionally kicking one of the many Norway Spruce fir cones which glistening wetly and dun brown in colour.

As the track rose, the densely planted fir trees at the side of the track thinned out at one point to afford me a view of the surrounding countryside. A swirling, white mist still lingered in the glen below me leaving the tops of the neighbouring hills appearing like barren grey-green islands in a milky-white sea. The rain of the previous evening had moved off to the east and the sky above was a cloudless blue. The entire picture through the gap in the pines was an incredibly beautiful, almost surrealist view. The heady, intoxicating scent of the pine trees, and the utter silence and solitude of the place, added greatly to the occasion. I do believe that if at that very moment my peace had been disturbed by the sudden arrival of fellow travellers along that track, I may have been tempted to commit murder.

I am not a very spiritual type of person, being both too thick and insensitive, but as I moved further along the track and the trees thinned out to leave me on the high, deserted moorland, I began to understand the power that the wildernesses and desolate places of the world have had on holy men of all persuasions. There was not a sound nor the merest sight of civilisation, just myself and my thoughts on the high, bare moorland.

This was the day of the royal wedding between Prince Andrew and Sarah Ferguson. Although I wished them all the best, as I would any newly wed couple, I could not help thinking to myself that I was in one of the best places to be that day. Up on this high plateau between the bulk of Beinn Liath Mhor and grey Carn Breac, I was strolling alongside the rushing, laughing waters of the river Coulin. Most importantly, I was miles away from the nearest television set covering the royal wedding. I had no doubt that the usual form of sycophantic inanities would be issuing forth as usually seemed to happenwhenever discussing the doings of the family Windsor.

The weather held fair all that morning, further spicing my enjoyment of the tranquillity and the scenery. Eventually I walked past the isolated Coulin lodge, the first sign of human habitation I had seen in over two hours. The track meandered on past the twin lochs of Coulin and Clair. Although these small lochs are both situated well inland, several miles from the sea, they are a popular roosting place for cormorants.

I spoke briefly with a visiting English angler who walked with me for half a mile or so, accompanied by his handsome, golden retriever which darted about among the gorse bushes looking hopefully for rabbits. He told me that he was up on holiday from Buckinghamshire, his wife and daughter had decided to stay in Kinlochewe that morning and watch the wedding, so he had taken the excuse to go fishing. A sensible man.

With a slight twinge of sadness, I finally left the forestry track and joined the main road in the shadow of brooding Beinn Eighe. After a short walk into the village of Kinlochewe, I searched out the local hotel where I treated myself to an excellent, if expensive, bar lunch. The hotel bar was quite crowded with visitors to the 10,000 acre Beinn Eighe nature reserve. Barbour jackets or anoraks, and green wellies seemed to be dress of the day.

The road out of Kinlochewe followed the shore of Loch Maree. Out on the ink-dark waters of the loch, small boats skimmed back and forth. Well equipped anglers were casting optimistically from the shallows and the narrow, pebble beaches. I recalled that I had read somewhere that as well as brown trout, the loch was inhabited by a unique type of char. Across on the northern shore I could plainly see the distinctive 3,217 feet mass of Slioch, surrounded by the dark green mass of Letterewe forest which is reputed to contain some of the most ancient oak woods in Scotland.

Despite quite heavy tourist traffic on the narrow lochside road, that afternoon's walk was almost as equally pleasant on the eye as had been the morning's magical trek.

Towards early evening I arrived and stopped briefly at Talladale which I had considered as a likely spot for overnight camping. The weather was still holding fair and I felt still full of walking, so after a brief rest and a bite to eat, I forged on. The road began to turn inland, leaving Loch Maree and the thickly wooded islands of Subhairin and Ruairidh Mor behind me. The scrubby growth at the roadside steadily developed into stands of old Scots pine and birch, as I moved on into the cool, green shadiness of Slatterdale forest.

Twisting and climbing the road led on until the Norway and Sitka spruce, and larch trees of Slatterdale began to steadily thin out and I found myself in rough, hill country once more, looking out onto the picturesque vista of the sinking sun shining on the waters of Loch Bad an Sgalaig. The traffic on the single track road was very light as it was now sometime after nine o'clock in the evening, and I decided that it was time that I looked for somewhere to camp for the night.

Out of curiosity I followed a short, sloping track which led off the main road, and I came upon a small, level plateau which overlooked the road and Loch Bad an Sgalaig. The soil was a bit shallow and stony, but otherwise I doubted if I would find a better place to camp for the night, so I unpacked my gear. I had just unrolled my bivouac, prior to erecting it, when I was inflicted by a sudden visitation from *Culicoides impunctatus*, or to put it in plain English. 'Bloody midges!'

Like anyone who has spent their lives in the north of Scotland, I have been plagued by midges many times during my life. From sudden, annoying attacks of them when as a young boy I would go fishing for trout on lochs Calder and Watten in Caithness, to more recent times being

. . . a sudden visitation from Culicoides impunctatus . . .

assailed as I worked on the peat banks in Shetland. But I honestly cannot remember a more concentrated and furious assault than the one to which I was subjected that evening as I struggled to erect the bivouac. Countless thousands of these tiny black demons would launch wave after wave of kamikaze attacks on any piece of exposed flesh. It still sets me itching just writing about it!

When I finally had the bivouac erected, I speedily crawled inside and tightly zipped the entrance. As I lay on my back, frantically scratching, it soon became apparent that quite a number of midges had become shut inside the bivvy with me. I lit up a cigarette and had my revenge, taking a great, malicious delight in fumigating the bivvy interior with huge puffs of tobacco smoke. Finally, with all my uninvited guests either dead of asphyxiation or too stupefied to be any bother, I hauled myself into my damp sleeping bag and was almost instantly asleep despite the hard ground underneath me. It had been a long day.

Wonder of wonders, it did not rain that night. When I awoke in the morning and failed to hear the all too familiar pattering on the bivvy roof, I almost thought that I had gone deaf, possibly caused by a side effect of extensive midge bites.

Unzipping the bivouac entrance I poked my head out to face the morning. With a sense of foreboding I could plainly see gathering phalanxes of dark grey clouds massing in the west over the Minch. It did not require an expert meteorologist to predict that some pretty foul weather was not very far off, and I began to hurriedly pack my gear, eager to be well on the road before it hit. A sharp, westerly breeze had already sprung up, but this had the advantage of grounding the midges and allowing me to strike the bivouac unmolested.

While packing my backpack I noticed that the long walk was beginning to show signs of wear and tear on various articles of clothing. Two pairs of socks had been reduced to a state more of holes than sock material, and I buried these under a small cairn of stones. I would love to think that they might be re-discovered by some archaeologist in the year 3000 or so, and the speculations that he might make about such a find. "Yes, obviously one of the more obscure religious rites of twentieth century man, etc. . . ."

To return briefly to the subject of midges though. It is perhaps worthwhile mentioning that these tiny insects were regarded as important enough to become the subject of a government sponsored special committee inquiry, not so very long ago. Experts have predicted that if some way could be found to control, or at least neutralize the midge pest, then the tourist trade on the west coast of Scotland, which is one of the principal forms of income nowadays, could improve by as much as thirty per cent.

With my pack on my back I headed off along the road past Loch Bad an Sgalaig. If the lighthouse had still been manned, I would have been paying a visit to Rubha Reidh that day. Instead, I set my target for Dundonnell at the head of Little Loch Broom.

The morning's walk began with a stroll through pretty Kerrydale. The shallow river Kerry was once renowned for its pearl-bearing mussels. By mid-morning I had arrived at the fishing village of Gairloch, which had a quiet, sleepy-Sunday atmosphere about the place. Hardly a soul stirred about the single street, and except for two aged lobster boats, the small harbour was empty. As I continued out of the village and along the A832 which followed the sandy shoreline of the Gair Loch, the bad weather promise of the early morning was fulfilled.

Sheets of rain blown by the now gale force westerly wind pelted me as I trudged through the barren, bleak country between Gair Loch and Loch Ewe. White horses rode on the surface of Loch Tollaidh, and as the road began to descend into Poolewe, the rain water streamed around my feet like a swift flowing, if very shallow, river.

One or two hardy souls were fishing on the river Ewe, determined to make the most of their holidays despite the foul weather. I hurried on past them and headed for the Poolewe Hotel where I knew I could find warmth, food and drink.

Three-quarters of an hour later, reluctant but refreshed, I hit the road once more. The driving rain had eased temporarily, but the sky overhead was still black and swollen with more and the bitterly cold west wind was blowing as strong as ever, directly into my face. About a mile from the hotel I passed Inverewe gardens where a steady stream of tourist cars were turning off the main road to visit the famous plantations created by Osgood Mackenzie back in the last century. The National Trust took over the responsibility for Inverewe shortly after the Second World War. As I walked past, shivering miserably in the teeth of the gale, I found it almost hard to believe that over on the other side of the wall which separated these magnificent gardens from me, was flourishing a profusion of sub-tropical plants, rhododendrons and azaleas.

On the outskirts of Tuirnaig the rain returned in the shape of a particularly heavy downpour which caused me to take shelter in a disused tower of sorts at the entrance of some kind of long abandoned military camp. Here I smoked a soggy cigarette and re-assessed my plans for the day before heading off during a lull in the rain, along the shore of Loch Ewe.

During my short stay in Portree, my hostess Thelma Budge had told me that a cousin of hers lived in the village of Aultbea which stands on the shore of Loch Ewe. Thelma's cousin, Andy Reid, was a Ministry of Defence policeman at the large NATO fuel depot based at Aultbea. Andy had been stationed up in Shetland at the same time I had been on the Muckle Flugga lighthouse. In those days he was based at the government installation at Collafirth. He was a keen CB radio enthusiast — and still is — and in the Shetland days I knew him better by his CB handle 'The Old Man of Hoy'. David Macdonald, one of my fellow lightkeepers on the Flugga, used to keep a CB radio out at the lighthouse, and we would often speak to the 'Old Man of Hoy' during the quiet night watches. Whilst I had been in Portree, Thelma 'phoned Andy and told him about my walk. He had replied that if I should be passing through Aultbea I was to be sure to look him up if I wanted a bed for the night. Although I had no intention of going there originally as the village was a bit off the road I was following, the thought of a warm bed instead of a sodden and gale lashed bivouac, persuaded me to forego my plans of making for Dundonnell, and so I turned off the main road and headed for Aultbea.

I mentioned earlier that there was a NATO fuel depot situated at Aultbea. This remote area has had a long association with the military, particularly the Royal Navy. During the Second World War, it was in the deep waters of Loch Ewe that the Russian bound convoys used to muster, prior to setting off on their perilous trips to Murmansk and Archangel.

To my annoyance I found that I had lost the Old Man of Hoy's address. This however provided me with a good excuse to visit the local Aultbea pub to have a pint of beer and ask around to find out where my planned host for the night lived.

In the public bar of the Aultbea Hotel, the 'Jock Tamson's bairn's syndrome' struck once more. Firstly the barman was a close family friend of some people who are very good friends of mine from Westerdale in Caithness, the small village in which I got married. In addition, one of the three regulars drinking in the bar came from Castletown, which is about six miles from my home town of Thurso. They all knew Andy Reid well, and one of them said that they thought he might be on shift at the present time, but he gave me the works telephone number so I could 'phone and find out. I 'phoned up, and right enough, Andy was on shift until ten o'clock that evening when he said he would meet me up at his house, and he gave me the address.

Come ten o'clock I made my way to Andy's house where he and his wife made me most welcome, and we chatted until quite late. Andy told me that he planned retiring shortly, and that he was going to go home to Orkney and take over the family croft on the island of Hoy. I told him that we would have to listen out for him on the CB radio on Stroma. I slept well that night, snug in the luxury of a warm, dry bed, lulled to sleep by the noise of the wind howling outside.

After a massive cooked breakfast the next morning, Andy insisted on giving me a lift along the road as far as Dundonnell. I did not argue about this, as it was from this point where I would have started that day had the weather not forced me to detour and find shelter in Aultbea. It would also bring me within walking distance of Ullapool where I needed to do some shopping, and most importantly, visit the bank and replenish my very low stock of cash. This day was a Friday so I had to arrive in Ullapool before the banks closed or I would be snookered until Monday morning.

The road out of Aultbea passed between steep sided hills and then followed the curve of Gruinard Bay, with the anthrax poisoned island of Gruinard looking deceptively green and wholesome in the early morning sunshine. Yesterday's foul weather had moved off in the early hours of the morning, gone to annoy somebody else. At about the time I am writing, there was a big attempt underway to decontaminate Gruinard island. I watched a helicopter regularly flying back and forth between the afflicted island and a large depot of chemicals and other stores, which had been set up on the mainland.

Andy dropped me off at the head of Little Loch Broom. I stood and waved farewell to him until he was out of sight, then I strode out along the road which ran alongside the Dundonnell river. The countryside had been pretty bleak and cheerless along the shore of Little Loch Broom, but here I found myself passing through a mixed woodland consisting of such native species as Scots pine, birch, alder, oak, rowan and hazel. Near Dundonnell House had been planted a more exotic variety of trees including limes, beeches, sycamores and chestnuts, amongst others which I did not recognize.

A short distance before the road along which I was walking, the A832, linked with the A835 at Braemore junction, I spotted a signposted pathway leading off through the trees from the side of a roadside car park. On consulting my map I discovered that this was the Corrieshalloch Gorge nature trail, and if I was to follow this route, I would save about two miles of road walking.

The beaten mud path wound through leafy woodland, with the occasional tree root protruding onto the path to trip up the unwary. All of a sudden the trees cleared and I came face to face with the ruggedly impressive Corrieshalloch Gorge, a deep cleft in the grey rock down which white water thundered as it plunged to sea level. The area around the gorge was thronged with tourists who were either busily snapping away with their cameras or trying to sum up enough courage to cross the precarious looking suspension bridge which spanned the deep, rocky chasm of the gorge.

Corrieshalloch proved to be an interesting diversion, but in next to no time I found myself back on the main road once more, Ullapool bound. Much to my surprise and dismay, I was to encounter some of the worst traffic on the entire leg of the west coast just on that particular stretch of road. The traffic was very bad and thundered past with so little consideration that more than once I was forced to leap onto the narrow verge of the Inverlael forest, in order to preserve my health and wellbeing.

I think that at this stage in my narrative, it is high time I mentioned a few of my own observations on this business of long distance road walking. Well everybody else who has written a similar type of book has done. Why should I miss out?

I had read, and had been told by several people before I set out, that long distance road walking is an entirely different discipline than hill walking or general cross country rambling. In the light of experience, I can heartily agree with them.

Although the road walker can generally cover far greater distances in a day's walking, the constant, merciless jarring of your feet on the hard, metalled surface of the road, can and does take its toll. Hence my famous eighteen mile toe, and the great relief I felt when I took my boots off for the night. The hill walker and the cross country rambler have the obstacles of streams, bogs, particularly rough or steep terrain, and other natural barriers to surmount; but the road walker has a far more deadly and calculating obstacle to contend with. Traffic!

In accordance with the Highway Code, I generally walked facing the oncoming traffic. This could be bad enough on busy roads, but at least you could see what was coming and have sufficient time to take the appropriate evasive action if necessary. The most frightening thing was when there was a car which was going in the same direction as you, decided to overtake. The sudden unexpected rush and zoom of something coming at your back, and more often than not passing by so close that you could reach out and touch it if you did not mind losing a hand, was enough to give you kittens.

I used to find that after a relatively short time of walking in really heavy traffic, the nervous exhaustion brought about by being forever on the alert, took more out of me than had I walked up to three times the distance on a quieter road. I quite often added several miles to my journey by taking the little used B roads and quiet country lanes in order to avoid the heavy traffic on the more direct main roads. I also found that after a day's walking in heavy traffic, I had worked myself into an almost pathological hatred of drivers. It was often that only a great deal of will-power and self-control prevented me from experiencing the sheer delight of picking up a brick or similar missile and hurtling it through the windscreen of the next approaching vehicle.

I observed that there were several different classifications of driver to be encountered on our roads. The principal and most common type of driver was the plain indifferent car owner who would usually just pass me by, politely and sensibly, pulling out slightly to give me room if the oncoming traffic allowed. Then there was the 'I've-got-a-car-and-you-are-just-a-bloody-pedestrian' type of driver, who would roar past indifferently, coming so close that the wind of their passing would almost bowl you into the ditch. Finally I found that the other common type was of the 'Hail-fellow-well-met' variety. These types were mainly tourists, and normally encountered on a day of pouring rain when I was squelching miserably along. From the warm, dry, secure comfort of their lemming-chariot, they would turn their smug, complacently beaming faces at me and bestow a cheery wave. I wonder if any of them ever stopped to wonder why the sopping wet hiker they had just passed was only waving back with two fingers.

. . . the sopping wet hiker . . . was only waving back with two fingers . . .

The majority of lorry drivers were gentlemen, although there was inevitably the odd one who fancied himself as Nigel Mansell. However, I found that the majority of bus and touring coach drivers came under the 'I've-got-a-bus/coach-and-you-are-just-a-bloody-pedestrian' classification.

By far the most considerate and friendliest drivers I met with were bikers. Rarely did a motorcyclist pass me by without a cheery wave or a dip of his headlight. This was not done out of patronisation or complacency, the biker and I had an affinity in foul weather. I recall at one point on the east coast, I was passed by a motorbike gang — the 'Pittenweem Sons of Satan' or suchlike — of about twenty-five bikers all driving in Indian file. By the time they had all sped past me, my arm was sore with returning salutes.

There was also the other type of biker, the touring cyclist. This happy breed provided me with endless entertainment and wonder. I would often see one of these cyclists with his bike laden and accoutred with side bags hanging over both front and back wheels; a bulging saddle bag; while the cyclist himself would be shouldering a backpack of gargantuan proportions, topped off with a rolled up tent or sleeping bag. Such well encumbered cyclists could occasionally be spotted straining every muscle in an attempt to surmount the slightest of gradients, their bikes weaving shakily all over the road. In fact on the Ullapool to Ledmore Junction stretch of road, walking at my normal pace, I actually overtook one such laden American cyclist, twice!

But, enough of this digression about traffic; back to the tale of the walk. By diligently pushing on that afternoon I succeeded in reaching Ullapool a good half hour before the banks closed for the day and the weekend. As if to congratulate me on my arrival, the sun was actually shining on the still waters of Loch Broom.

When I was in my late teens-early twenties, my cronies and myself living up in Thurso, would occasionally grab our camping gear, some food, and a large carry-out, pile into a couple of cars and head west. Ullapool was a popular stopping off place, and I happily recall some memorable times here which in those days were spent camping on a very rough and ready campsite on the shore of Loch Broom. This camping was usually free, or at the most cost a couple of tins of beer. The pubs were cheerful and friendly, and the Saturday night dances at the local hall were great fun. Sadly, since those days more and more tourists have discovered this delightful little town, and also taking into account the annual visits of the east European 'Klondykers', the good people of Ullapool seem to have become 'organized'. While it has spoiled the place for me, I cannot find it in myself to blame anybody. There is little enough employment in this corner of Ross-shire.

I found that the old campsite had changed beyond all recognition. There was now a high, wire fence completely encircling the place, an entrance gate where mixed fees for tents or caravans were collected and signposts stating in bold letters 'Beach parties prohibited'. The whole was laid out geometrically in neat camping areas, with all the adjacent facilities including a laundromat, shops, and a water tap exclusively for washing dirty dishes. Even the grass was neatly mown! I suppose it had to come, and it is what the hardy campers in their expensive caravans — colour T.V. optional — and caravanettes, like to expect when they rough it. But it was just a little bit saddening just the same.

The staff of the campsite were however kind enough to allow me free camping when I explained to them the point of my journey, and I confess that a good soak in the hot showers at the campsite, had the edge on the old practice of a quick dip in the icy cold waters of Loch Broom.

I spent a fairly quiet evening wandering around Ullapool, which was, as one local said to me, 'fair infested with tourists'. After an indifferent meal and a couple of pints of beer, I returned to the campsite and turned in for the night.

Although I was woken during the night by the sound of quite heavy rain, for some inexplicable reason my temperamental bivouac did not leak. I regarded this as a good omen, and I quite cheerfully packed my gear in the morning and headed off into town for breakfast.

In a nearby shop I purchased a couple of fresh rolls and a pint of milk which I polished off for breakfast while sitting on a public bench at the lochside and being entertained by the arrival, or was it departure, of the Stornoway ferry.

The road north out of Ullapool climbed with heartbreaking steepness before suddenly plunging down to Ardmair with its picturesque caravan site and boating centre. Out in the approaches to Loch Broom I could see the island of Martin which was once renowned for its herring curing station. The herring fishing in Loch Broom was once very prolific and was first discovered and exploited by the Dutch in the early 1700s. However, the British soon got wind of it and speedily drove off the Dutch herring busses. Curing stations were set up on Isle Martin and nearby Isle Tanera, where the fish were dried and cured before export to the West Indies and southern Ireland. Unfortunately this lucrative fishing industry died out as long ago as the 1880s.

The road headed steadily northwards, passing through grassy, green Strathkanaird, and skirting the heights of Coigach. This was sheep grazing country. Black faced ewes would stand on one side of the road bleating 'Baaaaairn', while their offspring stood on the opposite side plaintively crying in reply 'Maaaaaa', before deciding to take a quick rush across, usually in front of a frantically braking car.

From mid-morning onwards the weather began to alternate between sudden, short, sharp, squally showers of rain which gusted in off the Minch, and periods of blazing hot sunshine. The sun was so warm and the westerly wind was so brisk, that my clothing would be dried out completely within minutes, only to be soaked through again by the next passing shower.

I skirted the edge of the Cromalt hills, and passed both the Knockan Cliff nature trail and the Inverpolly nature reserve with its stands of rowan and birch trees in an almost treeless landscape. At the tiny village of Elphin I passed a double, major milestone, in that I estimated that I had now walked one thousand miles, and at the same time I had now passed into the county of Sutherland, next door neighbour to my home county of Caithness. When I saw the sign proclaiming this on the county boundary, I felt at last that I was really on the road home.

I had been expecting a village of sorts at Ledmore Junction, but the place was just as its name describes it, a junction of roads and nothing else. Here I joined the A837 which took me through the wild but scenic countryside to my final destination for that day — Inchnadamph.

The small public bar of the Inchnadamph Hotel was full of outdoor enthusiasts of varied persuasions; hill-walkers, climbers, amateur geologists, naturalists, ornithologists, fishermen, and a party of Venture Scouts who had been potholing in the limestone caves for which the area is noted. I found myself sat next to a local farmer, and we were soon discussing and comparing sheep farming in Caithness and Sutherland, and later he gave me a humorous account about the recent Inchnadamph sheep dog trials. Thinking that it was about time that I set up camp for the night, I asked him if there was anywhere nearby where I might pitch my bivouac, and he kindly gave me permission to use one of his fields which was conveniently adjacent to the hotel.

In no time I had my bivouac safely and securely erected in the shelter of a small copse of birch trees on the bank of the river Traligill which rushed down to Loch Assynt from the heights of Conival and Beinn More Assynt. For want of anything better to do, and a feeling that I should at least celebrate my thousand miles, I returned to the bar of the Inchnadamph Hotel. I spent a pleasant enough evening in the pub in the company of Bill and Hilda Sinclair from Turriff, who were on a hill walking holiday. They had been hoping to climb Beinn More Assynt but so far the weather had defeated them.

Needless to say that night the heavens opened up once more and my bivouac reverted back to its normal situation of leaking in a good half dozen places. I awoke in the early dawn feeling generally wet, cold, miserable, and wondering why the hell had I left Scrabster in the first place. In the drab, pale grey early morning light I packed my gear under the dripping branches of the birch trees. As I was making such an early start, I resolved that day I was going to make it to Kinlochbervie or bust. This was a distance of about thirty-two miles along a twisting, roller coaster of a road.

There was a good reason behind my eagerness to reach Kinlochbervie. Some good friends of mine lived there during the summer while they worked at the bag-net salmon fishing. Before I had set out on my walk, I had arranged to call on them and have a day off when I reached that part of the country. The knowledge that I was certain of a dry bed in the salmon fishing bothy that night should I reach Kinlochbervie helped to spur me on through the soaking showers and bitter wind which assailed me as I struck off along the shore of Loch Assynt.

As I rubbed the driving rain out of my eyes, I wondered if the Marquis of Montrose, a broken fugitive after the disastrous and ill-advised battle of Carbisdale, had been confronted by the same foul weather when he had arrived in Assynt and sought refuge with the treacherous local laird, Macleod of Assynt.

While I was walking past the impressive ruins of Ardvreck castle, a tourist bus suddenly appeared on what had been an otherwise completely trafficless road. The bus pulled in to a lay-by adjacent to the castle ruins and a horde of tourists poured out and braved the elements to take photographs of Ardvreck. This ruin on a small peninsula jutting out into Loch Assynt, used to be a famous nesting and breeding site of ospreys until the deprivations of 19th century egg collectors, and local shooting caused the last of these magnificent birds to be completely wiped out here in 1848.

It was only after the touring bus had moved off that I looked at my watch and noticed with some surprise that the time was only seven a.m. and this was a Sunday morning! I can only conclude that some tour operators and their patrons must be keener than others, or that the foul weather was beginning to give me hallucinations.

Forging ever northwards, I branched off the A837 which would lead eventually to the booming west coast fishing port of Lochinver, and took to the A894, the road which I would follow all the way to Laxford Bridge.

This road steadily snaked and climbed through a wild country carpeted with coarse, poor grass which was scattered with the eruptions of craggy protuberances of rock which appeared to sprout through the thin soil as if carelessly planted there. I had been told by one of the amateur geologists in the Inchnadamph Hotel bar the previous evening, that this type of rock was very ancient and known as Lewisian gneiss of Precambrian age, dated at more than 1,500 million years old. No it did not mean a great deal to me either, but seemingly these rocks, and the Torridonian sandstone, slightly younger at 800 million years of age, account for much of the underlying strata of this barren and empty northwest corner of Britain.

As the road flattened out at the summit, the weather cleared briefly to present me with a magnificent view of the almost barbaric splendour of the rugged country around me. At my left shoulder reared the bare hills of Quinag, Sail Gharbh and Sail Ghorm; in front of me was laid out an unchanging, yet ever different, landscape of short, faded, green grass littered with boulders and rocky outcrops and leading down to the blue-grey waters of the sea loch Loch Cairnbawy, which merged with Loch Glendhu and Loch Glencoul where the waters narrowed at the site of the old Kylesku ferry.

After negotiating the steady descent down the hill, I stopped briefly for my first rest of the day at Kylesku. I sat on the wall by the scenic little harbour, crowded with small lobster fishing boats. Two anglers from Dundee were trying their luck on the loch with spinning rods. One of the two proudly told me that he had caught three excellent sea-trout from this very spot on the previous day, and he was hoping to bag more before he had to return home to his work in the city. I sincerely wished him luck, having an instinctive streak of sympathy in me for anybody who lives in Dundee.

Leaving Kylesku I crossed the waters by way of the impressive new road bridge, financed with Common Market money, which has at long last made the ferry redundant. Once across the bridge, a heavy shower of rain accompanied me for most of the way along the kelp encrusted shore of Eddrachillis Bay and on to the village of Scourie.

It had been my original plan to camp overnight at Scourie, but the sight of the rain sodden tents on the campsite helped to give an added spring to my step and stiffened my resolve to reach Kinlochbervie by evening.

At Laxford Bridge, the clouds unexpectedly cleared away and a hot, yellow sun blazed down from a clear blue sky, causing twisting tendrils of steam to rise off the wet road. I sat on the stone parapet of the bridge and smoked a cigarette while looking down contemplatively on the rain-swollen waters of the river Laxford. This river used to be famous for its pearl-bearing freshwater mussels, and was once regularly fished for them by itinerant tinkers. The tinker pearl fishermen would quarter the shallow, swift flowing river, peering at the bottom through a glass bottomed bucket or box. When a likely looking mussel, or one with the distinctive pearl scar on the shell, was spotted, they would loosen it from the river bed with a specially notched stick, and with one swift movement, whip it into the sack which they would carry slung over their shoulder.

To my delight the weather continued to hold fine as I walked through the rugged, wild country, along a narrow single track road. Over to the east of me I could clearly see the bare Cambrian quartzite summits of the two mountains which lent their names to two famous racehorses: the incomparable Arkle, and the lucky Grand National outsider, Foinavon.

At the small village of Rhiconich I turned off the road I had been following for the past couple of hours to head along the shore of Loch Inchard and on to the target destination of the day, Kinlochbervie.

The village of Kinlochbervie, or KLB as it sometimes get called, is situated on a narrow isthmus of land between two sea lochs. Loch Inchard is on the south side of the village, and the smaller Loch na Claise (Loch Clash, to the fishermen) is to the north. The two natural harbours formed by these lochs have long provided shelter for fishermen on this exposed and inhospitable northwest coast, but since the discovery of the rich fishing grounds around Rockall, this normally quiet little Sutherlandshire village had become something of a fishing boom town.

Many of the east coast based trawlers land their fish and take on ice and provisions at Kinlochbervie, rather than make the long trip to their home ports via the Pentland Firth. Frequently the trawlers are left for the weekend at their berths in Loch Inchard, while the crews head off in hired minibuses and taxis for their homes in Peterhead, Buckie, Fraserburgh and Lossiemouth.

It was a Sunday evening when I arrived, and I was passed on the road by several cars and minibuses full of returning fishermen. From the high ground above Kinlochbervie, I had a clear view of Loch Inchard, and I watched at least nine trawlers put out to sea in the time it took me to descend the hill into the village, and there were still another nine trawlers tied up at the quayside awaiting the arrival of their crews.

I felt weary and a bit footsore, but I was delighted at having reached my objective for the day, and I whistled cheerfully to myself as I strolled down to the wooden salmon fishing bothy perched on the shore of Loch na Claise. It was in this sea loch where the small fishing boat *Bon Ami* was so

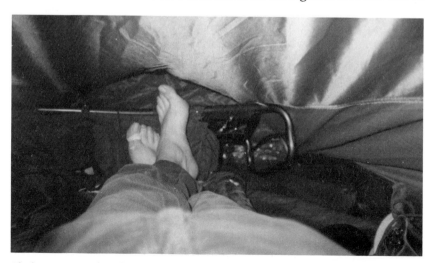

The bivouac interior and abused feet

tragically lost with all hands the previous year. My friends with whom I intended staying, Pete Keddy and Andy Wilcox, rent the salmon fishing rights on Loch na Claise from the Duke of Westminster (he probably needs the money). They told me that they still came across sad reminders of the shipwreck, in the shattered wood and fitments from the *Bon Ami* which occasionally became entangled in their nets.

According to the law of the land, the leader nets which direct the salmon into the bag-nets, have to be dismantled from midday Saturday until six o'clock Monday morning. As this was a Sunday, I knew that I would be more than likely to find my friends in the bothy enjoying their day off.

I entered the bothy and discovered that other visitors had arrived before me. I was delighted and surprised when I discovered their identity. These were Alan Parkinson, better known as 'Panz', and his girlfriend Mary. Panz and I had been great friends in our younger days in Thurso, and we had been mutually involved in numerous escapades. He had moved to work down in London where he was making a living as a motorbike despatch rider, a short time before I had left for Shetland. In consequence it was about eight years since we had seen each other. Panz's girlfriend was a native north Londoner, and the pair of them were on their summer holidays, slowly touring around the north coast of Scotland on their way to Thurso, where they finally ended up staying with me at Holborn Head for a week or so before heading back to the metropolis. By popular consent we all headed off to the Garbet bar in the Kinlochbervie Hotel for a reunion.

I enjoyed a long lie the next morning, making the most of a comfortable night spent in the warm, dry, bothy bunk-bed. When I eventually forced myself to face the day, I headed for the new Fisherman's Mission which was situated on the nearby quayside. Here I made use of the excellent shower facilities washing away the grime of travelling and clearing up my reunion hangover. By the time I returned to the bothy, Pete and Andy had come back in the coble after checking the nets. The strong wind that weekend had prevented them from complying with the law and taking in the leaders on Saturday. This meant that the nets had been fishing all weekend, and with the strong westerly winds often being concurrent with a big run of salmon on Loch na Claise, they had set out that morning full of optimism of a bumper catch.

Alas, out of the six bag-nets they had fished a meagre six salmon. Pete told me ruefully that this had not been a good season, and after paying for the equipment, fuel, food and rent, they would be lucky to break even. This was the same story I was to hear from all but one of the north Sutherland and Caithness salmon fishing stations.

That afternoon quite an amusing incident occurred. The salmon fishermen were busily doing some maintenance on the coble down at the lochside and Panz and Mary had gone off for an afternoon's walk. I was the only one left in the bothy, where I was sitting reading a book and generally enjoying being idle for the day. It was quite a hot day and I had left the bothy door wide open to provide some cool ventilation. Suddenly I was distracted from my reading by the sound of some tourists approaching the bothy. One of the tourists stood in the open doorway and asked me in a broad Birmingham accent, what kind of building was this place. I replied that it was a salmon fishing bothy, to which he quite reasonably inquired if I was a salmon fisherman. "No," I said. "I am a lighthouse keeper."

The inquisitive tourist snorted angrily at my reply, rapidly spun around on his heel and left to rejoin his companions. As they walked away I could distinctly hear him saying in aggrieved tones: "Sarcastic bugger! I was only asking him a polite question!"

. . . 'Sarcastic bugger!' . . .

Sadly, the time in Kinlochbervie passed all too quickly. I could willingly have stayed a week or longer, but with the arrival of Tuesday morning I had to be on the road once more. As I had already walked along the road into the village, and strictly speaking Kinlochbervie was a detour of several miles off my route, I accepted a lift from Panz into Rhiconich which was to be the starting point of my day's hike.

I walked through the same kind of wild, rugged, rocky country which I had been encountering every day of my walking in the north west. I will agree that this kind of country has a wild beauty of a unique kind and to spend a day travelling through it in a car can be quite captivating, nevertheless after you have been walking through the same landscape for a week it begins to get a little boring. To counteract this tedium I managed for the first time in days to obtain suitable radio reception on my backpack transistor radio, and Radio Scotland helped me along the road. However, the radio weather reports of heavy rain expected in the far north did little to encourage me.

During the rest day which I had spent at Kinlochbervie, the weather had been brilliantly sunny. It was probably the only day without at least one shower of rain since I had left Lochgilphead a fortnight previously. For some quite illogical reason this state of affairs had really annoyed me at the time. It was as if I had been allotted a certain number of dry days, and here was one of them turning up while I was taking my ease in the sheltered comfort of the salmon fishing bothy, instead of manifesting itself during a hard day's slog through open country. The salmon fishing crew had sat chuckling in amusement as I had stood in the bothy doorway exclaiming in rage and exasperation at the clear, blue sky: "It's my day off! Why isn't it bloody raining?"

After a while the course of the road which I was following joined and ran parallel to the river Dionard. I seemed to notice a fisherman every hundred yards or so on the river bank, all enthusiastically thrashing the water with their fly fishing lines. A short distance before the point where the Dionard flows into the Kyle of Durness, I stopped and watched one delighted angler land a very handsome sea trout.

In the early afternoon I stopped for sandwiches at the Cape Wrath Hotel. This was situated about a quarter of a mile from the ferry landing where I would take the boat over the blue waters of the Kyle to join the road which would lead me to Cape Wrath lighthouse where I intended spending the night. The hotel bar was full of anglers, and I chatted to a few of them over a pint of beer. They were quite a cosmopolitan crew, having come from all parts of Britain, and a few from Europe, to enjoy the excellent fishing to be had around these parts.

The small ferry boat which crosses the Kyle of Durness, operates in conjunction with two minibuses which transport tourists up to the lighthouse at Cape Wrath. The popularity of this service quite surprised me, and it was some time before I managed to cross over myself, leaving behind me on the east shore of the Kyle, quite a substantial number of newly arrived tourists awaiting their turn to be ferried over.

The local ferryman had heard all about my walk and had been half expecting me any day now. He carried me over free of charge and lamented to me about the large number of tourists who had been wanting to make the trip across over the course of the past few weeks. I commented that he must be making plenty of money with so many full busloads, and looking at me with an expression of rueful reflection, he sighed: "Ach yes, there is the money. But man, the harassment! The harassment!"

Having been earlier informed (erroneously as I found out later), that I was not allowed to travel by foot up to the lighthouse because the road passed through a RAF low-flying and bombing range, I boarded the minibus along with the tourists for the short run up to Cape Wrath.

Although the name 'Cape Wrath' sounds eminently suitable in describing this wild, remote headland with cliffs which rear up to 450 feet, and at one point are as high as 600 feet. The vegetation is officially described as sub-arctic, and a bird more common to the high mountain tops, the ptarmigan, breed here nearer the sea than anywhere else in the country. The word 'Wrath' has absolutely nothing to do with wild ferocity or anger, but is a corruption of the Norse word 'Hvarf' which translated into English simply means 'turning point'. A term which adequately described to the Norsemen in their longships where the north coast of Scotland ended and they could turn sharp left to head off down the Minch for the summer raiding and pillaging among the Hebrides and Ireland.

The building of a lighthouse in this remote corner of Britain was first proposed in 1802 after the loss in a severe storm off the Cape of three ships, out of which only two men survived. The Northern Lighthouse Board was heavily committed at the time and it was not for another twenty-five years before work began, and the light was finally established in 1828.

Of all the mainland lighthouses which I visited during the course of my walk, Cape Wrath was the only lighthouse which was classified as a relieving station. That is to say that the men who manned the lighthouse here worked the same kind of routine as lightkeepers on an offshore lighthouse. They have four weeks on duty at the lighthouse, followed by four weeks off duty at the lighthouse shore station, which is situated in Golspie, Sutherlandshire. The reason why this routine is worked at a mainland station, is because of the particular remoteness of Cape Wrath. As well as the obvious problem of children's schooling, it would be unfair to ask a lightkeeper's family to live permanently in such an out of the way spot. However, not so many years ago this was the case.

I disembarked from the minibus to find throngs of bemused tourists wandering around the lighthouse perimeter, busily snapping away with their cameras every few minutes. I entered the accommodation building where I found the three besieged lightkeepers watching television.

Principal lightkeeper Donald Macleod was known to me of old. Donald has the dubious distinction of being the first principal lightkeeper I was to work under with the Northern Lighthouse Board. He was in charge of the lighthouse at Niest Point on Skye when I was sent there as a supernumary lightkeeper under training.

After a chat, Donald kindly cooked some tea for me, and then fixed me up with one of the spare bedrooms for the night. After a hot shower to

Cape Wrath
courtesy of Christopher Nicholson

remove the daily grime generated by road walking, I settled down for a quiet, restful night in front of the television.

I slept well that night in the room which was normally occupied by assistant lightkeeper Tom Scott who was off duty in Golspie. I must be making a habit of taking over Tom's beds, as he was the lightkeeper who I replaced in Stroma. After a very substantial breakfast the next morning, assistant lightkeeper Alec Dorricot gave me a lift down to the ferry landing in the lighthouse Land Rover. The ferryman was busy transporting tools and equipment back and forth for the County Council road workers, and I was his only passenger on the return journey. Although as we landed, I noticed the first of the day's tourists beginning to turn up.

I noticed that the tide was out in the Kyle and the colour of the exposed sands was a deep, golden, picture-postcard yellow which helped to brighten up the drabness of the dull green colouring of the surrounding countryside.

After a short walk I arrived in Durness where I visited the local general store and grocers to replenish my iron rations of oatcakes and corned beef, also buying half a dozen apples to eat on the road. The Durness campsite was packed with colourful tents and I was passed by several tourists on their way to explore the famous Smoo caves on the outskirts of Durness.

Rabbits scampered about the gorse bushes lining the road which took me along the shore of Loch Eriboll. As I walked, I could plainly see both the long, straight road which stretched out ahead of me leading to the head of the sea loch, and across the water in plain view was the road along which I would have to travel later that day. This was a frustrating experience but one which I had long become used to on the western seaboard of Scotland which is indented with sea lochs. It was a situation which often made me wish that I had carried a small, inflatable boat on my backpack. I would have saved miles of walking.

Traffic was fairly light on the single track road along the loch side, and but for snatches of birdsong and the occasional plaintive bleat of a black-faced sheep, there was little noise to disturb the peace of the day. This would not have been the case for the space of a couple of weeks some forty odd years ago when the quiet sea loch of Loch Eriboll would have echoed and resounded with the growl of aircraft engines and the crump of practice bombs. Because of the loch's similarity to a Norwegian fjord, it was in Loch Eriboll where the British aircraft practised their bombing runs before going off to do the real thing on the Nazi warship Tirpitz.

Near the head of the loch and birch wood dotted Strath Beag, I spotted a flash of movement in the still, dark waters, as a fully grown female grey seal lifted her head out of the water to peer at me for a moment before quickly submerging and swimming away. I had been told that quite a large colony of grey seals bred in the sea caves which are scattered along the shores of Loch Eriboll. Still on the subject of seals, once I had cleared the Loch Eriboll region I walked past Loch Hope. Now although this is not a sea loch, I was told that seals are quite often spotted swimming about in the peat brown water. Not the nervous, man-fearing grey seals, but the smaller common or harbour seal. It is thought that they occasionally swim up the short length of the river Hope and into the loch in pursuit of fish.

After taking most of the day just to walk round Loch Eriboll, it was already early evening by the time I began to traverse the bleak moorland expanse of A Mhoine, but there was absolutely nowhere suitable to camp in this barren, desolate region of rock and peat bog. Having little choice I resolved to push on to the village of Tongue and either camp there or somewhere in the general area.

The drab grey of the sky was beginning to darken and merge with the washed out grey-green of the moorland when I topped a rise and finally spotted in the near distance the orange pinpoints of light which shone in Tongue.

I had thought that I knew a good campsite on this shore of the Kyle of Tongue, but by the time I arrived at the water's edge it had become too dark to go wandering along the Kyle shore looking for the place which I had in mind. Wearily I pushed on following the road onto the causeway which crossed the Kyle, hoping to find somewhere to camp near the village. As things turned out, I did not have to travel far. The causeway across the Kyle of Tongue passes through two small islands, and on the first of these I came across a large lay-by, at the rear of which was a sizeable expanse of flat grassland, screened from the road by gorse bushes and bracken.

As soon as I had the bivvy erected I crawled inside and fell upon the corned beef and oatcakes bought in Durness that morning. I ravenously devoured all but a small portion of this food, which along with my last apple, I kept for breakfast the following morning. I had completed another thirty plus miles and I was soon wrapped up in my sleeping bag and sound asleep.

The all too familiar sound of heavy rain, and the dripping of the Chinese water torture of rainwater leaking through the bivouac roof onto my sleeping bag woke me early the next morning. I did not need to look outside, or muster too much imagination to realize that this was a particularly filthy morning. After a wait of about an hour which I spent huddled in the driest part of the bivouac, eating my breakfast, the situation showed little sign of improving. With a reluctant sigh of acceptance, I struggled into my waterproofs, and after first packing evrything into my backpack, I crawled outside and hastily struck down the bivouac.

It was only six thirty in the morning and the village of Tongue was not yet fully awake as I trudged - or rather squelched - through the streets streaming with water. Sometime during the night the prevailing westerly wind had completely changed to blow from the east, and steadily blew wave after wave of rain and drizzle into my face.

Some miles past Tongue I took a brief respite at the village of Coldbackie, where I noticed that even the normally beautiful golden

sands of the beach there looked washed out and miserable. Here I came
upon a public 'phone box in which I managed to jam myself and backpack
and enjoyed a smoke in the dry for ten minutes.

Pushing on I headed past Borgie Forest. As the road ascended past the
drooping, dripping trees, it took on the appearance of a shallow river with
my feet splashing through at least an inch of fast flowing rainwater which
the ditches on either side of the road could no longer cope with. By this
time it had already penetrated my boots to add to my general discomfort.
A day of this weather was far too grey and miserable to show up the scenic

. . . a smoke in the dry for ten minutes . . .

beauty of Strath Naver at its best, and as I crossed the bridge over the river Naver at Bettyhill, my destination for that day, the rain hissed on the swollen waters below like steam.

The Bettyhill Hotel, a place I knew well of old, was a more than welcome sight, and my pace quickened as I headed for the public bar and a seat in the dry. Shrugging off my water streaming backpack and waterproofs, I enjoyed a bar lunch of chicken curry washed down with two glasses of rum and at last began to feel the warmth returning to my benumbed body, if not the dryness. Looking out through the bar window, I could plainly see that the weather showed little sign of easing up, and I began to ponder on the problem of where I was going to spend the night. Another soaking in the bivouac did not appeal, though I suppose I should have been getting used to it by now. Just at that moment I heard a surprised voice address me by name, and I looked up to see on the other side of the bar, the pretty, petite figure of Lindsay Holmes, an old friend of mine who lived a couple of miles outside of Bettyhill at her mother's house in the village of Kirtomy.

Lindsay told me that she was working part time in the hotel during the tourist season, and as she had just finished for the day she came round and joined me. A short while later we were joined by her brother Philip, who with Lindsay's other brother Julian, worked the bag-net salmon fishing station at nearby Port Vasgo. Philip had come to drive Lindsay home to Kirtomy, and they both urged me to come along, assuring me that their mother would be delighted to put me up for the night.

Kip Holmes did not bat an eyelid when she saw the bedraggled, soaking figure that her offspring had brought home with them. I had met Kip once or twice before and had taken an instant liking to her. A fine intelligent lady, full of fun. She made me very welcome.

A steaming hot bath soon dispelled the miseries of the day's walk, and the remainder of the day passed all too quickly in such excellent company. That night I savoured the luxury of a warm, dry sleep on the living room couch. The situation was made all the more delightful as I enjoyed the heat and glow from the blazing peat fire in the grate, and listened to the noisy rattle of the wind and rain on the crofthouse windows.

When I arose in the morning I discovered that the foul weather had blown itself out and the sun was shining weakly through a thin covering of dirty white clouds. The early morning weather forecast on Radio Scotland was less than inspiring though, forecasting a return of the heavy rain that evening. After saying my farewells, I walked along the quiet back roads out of Kirtomy, munching away on one of the bananas which Kip had insisted that I take with me for sustenance on the road.

After a walk of two miles or so, I rejoined the main road and pushed on eastwards. I was virtually on home territory now and I knew the area well.

By midday I had reached the village of Strathy where I stopped briefly before turning off the road and heading for Strathy Point and the final lighthouse on my check-off list.

The road up to Strathy Point lighthouse was a narrow, single track road which passed one or two scattered croft houses, a salmon fishing station, and numerous grazing sheep. These were all situated on the thin finger of barren rocky land which juts out into the Pentland Firth. I looked east across the expanse of Strathy Bay and I could clearly see the jumble of factory like buildings and the distinctive, spherical, light-blue painted dome of the Dounreay atomic research establishment. This familiar sight, probably more than any other, really brought home to me the fact that the following day I would at last be home, and my long trek would be over.

Although it had not been deliberately planned this way, Strathy Point lighthouse was strangely appropriate and fitting to be the final lighthouse which I was to call at. Strathy Point lighthouse had been built as recently as 1958, and was the last, major, manned lighthouse to be established by the Northern Lighthouse Board. Strathy was also the very first lighthouse to be constructed with an all electric power system. This in itself heralded

Strathy Point lighthouse
courtesy of Northern Lighthouse Board

the dawn of a new age in lighthouse technology which over the years since has provided the means to slowly but inevitably make more and more lighthouses automatic and completely independent of the many lightkeepers who have tended them over the past two hundred years.

I did not linger overlong at Strathy Point — just staying long enough for a cup of tea and a short chat with assistant lightkeeper Jim Craigie who signed my check-in sheet. Leaving the place behind me, I slowly and thoughtfully strolled off back along the road in the anticlimax of the realization that I had just successfully completed my lighthouse walk.

The village of Melvich was to be my destination for that day, and it was not a long walk from Strathy. I knew the landlord of the Croft Inn at Melvich, he greeted me when I arrived in his pub, and kindly gave me permission to put up my bivouac in his field at the rear of the Croft Inn.

That evening I entered the pub bar with the original intention of celebrating the completion of my walk, but with mixed feelings I discovered that my heart was just not in it, and I left early for the last night in my bivouac and soggy sleeping bag.

The final day dawned as had so many before in the past couple of weeks, with torrential rain. I had long found that the top end of my bivouac did not leak and I squeezed myself up into this one dry spot where I sat on my backpack disconsolately chain smoking and waiting for the weather to ease up. It didn't, in fact if anything the rain got even heavier. The weeks of rain had by this time completely demoralized me and I was heartily sick of walking through soaking wet weather, wearing soaking wet clothes, and sleeping in a soaking wet sleeping bag in a soaking wet tent. I decided there and then that the Scottish mainland lighthouse walk was officially over. I had completed my objective of walking round all the manned mainland lighthouses on my arrival at Strathy Point the previous day. Although for the sake of a tidy finish if nothing else, I would have liked to have walked the final twenty miles to Scrabster, the weather had at last become too much and I could see no dishonour in catching the midday bus to Thurso.

Since the day I had left Holborn Head lighthouse, fifty-eight days previously, I estimated that taking into account my trip along the border from east coast to west, and my occasional island hopping and deviations from the planned route, I had covered a distance in excess of 1,300 miles of which at least 1,100 had been travelled on foot. For those who like numerical statistics this would have amounted to some 1,187,000 paces and a total force absorbed by my body of 300,000 tons. Also during the course of the walk I had been sunburned, blistered, half-drowned and half-frozen, severely bitten by midges and severely harassed by traffic and dogs, hungry and hungover, but I would not have missed it for the world, it had been the experience of a lifetime.

Many people who I met on my travels expressed their surprise that I had no back-up team accompanying me. In answer to this I am tempted to quote Rudyard Kipling:

> 'Down to Gehenna or up to the Throne,
> He travels fastest who travels alone.'

However, I did always regard the lighthouses which I visited as a back-up organization of sorts, and although it may sound like a patronising cliche I had the best back-up team in the world in the ordinary people of Scotland, who from Dunnet Head to Mull of Galloway treated me with such friendliness and unsought kindness.

I took down and packed the bivvy for the last time, then strolled across to the main road and caught the midday bus. As the bus drove past the 'split-stane' on the outskirts of Melvich and the ancient boundary marker between the counties of Caithness and Sutherland, I looked out of the window on familiar if sopping wet country.

Three quarters of an hour later I alighted from the service bus at the turn-off road for Scrabster, walking the last mile and a half into the village.

My first stop was at the house of my friend Jenny Sutherland. Jenny had been looking after my cross-collie bitch Storm, while I had been away. Judging by Storm's thickening girth, she had been well looked after in my absence, and we were both glad to see each other.

Contemplatively I strolled the last half mile or so through Scrabster, heading for my home at Holborn Head. On the way I bumped into one of the local worthies who silently eyed me up and down before commenting: "So you made it then?" "Aye, I made it," I replied. "Mmmm," he sighed, "I suppose you will be off on a bloody lap of honour next week!"

Postscript

 The following is a list of the equipment and general gear which I carried around with me on the walk:

'Campari' bivvy bivouac. (I took great delight in burning this the day after I had returned home at Holborn Head)
Sleeping bag (still giving sterling service)
'Philips' transistor radio
Tobacco tin containing plasters, needle and thread, aspirins, alka-seltzer, etc.
Bible
Sheaf of pertinent AA road maps torn out of AA road atlas
5 pairs of thin ankle socks
3 pairs of thick sea-boot stockings
4 pairs of Y-fronts
1 heavy lumberjack type shirt
3 T-shirts (2 more acquired off the RNLI in Edinburgh)
1 lambswool jumper
1 pair tracksuit trousers
1 pair of old corduroy trousers. (Became indecent by the time I had reached Aberdeen, so scrounged another pair off my brother)
1 pair of shorts
2 towels
variety of minor miscellaneous items such as tooth brush, boot dubbin etc.

I rarely carried food except on the more remote stretches of the west coast when I would carry iron rations of corned beef and oatcakes. Occasionally I would purchase glucose tablets or chocolate to eat on the road, and the odd bottle of lemonade or lucozade. The boots I wore were of an Italian make and stood up to the journey remarkably well. The bulk of the wear sustained by them was at the heels which by the end of the walk had worn away to almost nothing.

In the light of experience, if I was ever to do this type of thing again, I would dispense with the bivouac and rely solely on bed and breakfast, and friends and acquaintances.

I think that the initial aim of using this walk to promote the Northern Lighthouse Board's bi-centenary, proved quite successful, as the walk generated quite a lot of interest and publicity in local and national Scottish newspapers. It was also widely reported on local radio and twice narrowly missed appearing on TV.

From the fund raising point of view, I would like to think that was also a success. A couple of months after my return home I received a letter from the RNLI saying that over £1,700 had been collected, and as I personally know of several cases where the money collected was donated directly to local lifeboat organizations rather than sent directly to Edinburgh, I would hazard a guess that the total raised was in excess of £2,000.

A particular thank you should be mentioned to my local, the Scrabster Hotel where over £300 was raised; the personnel of the Northern Lighthouse Board who as well as making the whole enterprise possible, also gave very generously; the generous donation received from Shetland, which as I have said did not even feature on my journey; and finally just to everybody who helped, aided, assisted, or put up with me during the walk.

Afterword

MUCH water has flowed past the lighthouse since the day I arrived back at Holborn Head after my marathon walk.

My walk may have finished that day, but the relentless march of demanning and automation has gone on steadily over the years. Of the twenty mainland lighthouses which I visited, at only four of them today will you see a lightkeeper. Holborn Head became fully automated with the retiral of Len Fraser in 1987; Dunnet Head was automated two years later in 1989. Duncansby Head is still manned but with a reduced crew. Noss Head was demanned and fully automated 1987; Covesea Skerries is still a holiday home for lightkeepers; Kinnaird Head was demanned and fully automated in 1991 and is now a national lighthouse museum. Buchan Ness was completely demanned in 1987 on the retiral of John Malcolm. Girdle Ness, was demanned and fully automated in 1991. Tod Head in 1988 and Scurdie Ness in 1987. Barns Ness was demanned before I arrived there (1985) and St. Abbs Head finally went in 1993.

There are no manned lighthouses on the Rinns of Galloway any more, Killantringan being automated in 1987, Mull of Galloway in 1988, and Corsewall in 1994. The lightkeepers left Turnberry in 1987, but at the time of writing the Mull of Kintyre is still manned. In 1988 Ardnamurchan was demanned. Cape Wrath and Strathy lighthouses are both still manned at the time of writing.

Other changes have of course come about; of the lightkeepers mentioned in this book many have retired, taken early retirement, and others such as John Lamont, have sadly passed away.

There has also been a lot of changes in my own life. Three years after the walk I re-married and my daughter Roxanne now has two young brothers, Liam and Robert. In 1993 I left the lighthouse service myself and settled in Scrabster.